THE DISCIPLING CYCLE SERIES

Understanding God

Andy and Kim Harrison

LifeWay Press®
Nashville, TN

ISBN 0-6330-3539-4

This book is a resource in the Personal Life-Youth
category of the Christian Growth Study Plan.
Course CG-0629
Dewey Decimal Classification Number: 231
Subject Heading: GOD–ATTRIBUTES

Printed in the United States of America.

Student Ministry Publishing
One LifeWay Plaza
Nashville, TN 37234-0174

We believe the Bible has God for its author; salvation for its end; and truth,
without any mixture of error, for its matter and that all Scripture is totally true
and trustworthy. The 2000 statement of *The Baptist Faith and Message* is our
doctrinal guideline.

Unless otherwise indicated, Scripture quotations are from the *New American
Standard Bible,* © Copyright The Lockman Foundation, 1960, 1962, 1963, 1968, 1971,
1972, 1973, 1975, 1977.
Used by permission.

Scripture quotations marked (NIV) are from the Holy Bible,
New International Version. Copyright © 1973, 1978, 1984 by International Bible Society.
Used by permission.

To order additional copies of this resource: WRITE LifeWay Church Resources
Customer Service, One LifeWay Plaza, Nashville, TN 37234-0113;
FAX order to (615) 251-5933; PHONE 1-800-458-2772;
E-MAIL to CustomerService@lifeway.com; ONLINE at *www.lifeway.com;*
or visit the LifeWay Christian Store serving you.

Art Direction & Designs: Edward Crawford

CONTENTS

THE AUTHORS

Andy Harrison serves as student ministry and education specialist for the Baptist General Convention of Oklahoma. Andy is a graduate of Oklahoma Baptist University and attended Southwestern Baptist Theological Seminary.

Andy and Kim ministered together on staff in the local church for nearly two decades. It was during that time they developed The Discipling Cycle for their own students.

The Harrisons strongly believe that the years of adolescence are crucial in grounding students in the Word of God and in the spiritual disciplines of the faith. It is their hope that the curriculum provided in The Discipling Cycle will encourage biblical discipleship in the church.

This book is dedicated to John Hatfield and Gerald Tidwell. They "have given of their lives to love and disciple us."

FOREWORD

Jesus has commanded in the Great Commission to "Therefore go and *make disciples* of all nations, baptizing them in the name of the Father and of the Son and of the Holy Spirit, and *teaching them to obey everything I have command-ed you . . .*" (Matt. 28:19-20a emphasis mine). Youth ministries in our country today have often failed at this task, not because the kids are unwilling, but be-cause we as leaders have under challenged them. I have found that youth re-spond to a challenge more deeply and with greater sacrifice than any age group I know. With this shared conviction, Andy & Kim Harrison have devel-oped The Discipling Cycle.

This book is more than a series of Bible studies, it is a pattern and plan for the challenge of youth discipleship. From the commitment to prayer for adult leaders to the one-on-ones with students, The Discipling Cycle presents a Christlike model for discipling youth. The Bible studies themselves are deeper in focus than much of the youth curriculum published today and consistently confront the student with Christ Himself.

The Discipling Cycle is designed to use the Word of God, prayer, and the con-sistent love of a discipling leader to challenge good students to become godly ones; ones able to internalize 2 Timothy 2:2, "The things you have heard me say in the presence of many witnesses entrust to reliable men who will also be qualified to teach others."

This program ought to be in every church and I challenge you to challenge your students and watch them grow "in wisdom and stature, and in favor with God and men."

Henry T. Blackaby

INTRODUCTION

Welcome to *The Discipling Cycle Series*, a three-year course designed to help develop strong, biblical discipleship in your church. This book is titled *Understanding God*, and is one of three books in this series. Each book represents 30 weeks of in-depth Bible study. The other two books are *Becoming Christlike* and *Seek, Share, Serve*. Each of these books also includes 30 weeks of study to help students become equipped in personal Bible study, Scripture memory, and practical life applications. *Becoming Christlike* focuses on internal transformation. *Seek, Share, Serve* focuses on evangelism, outreach, and discipleship. A Leader's Guide is available for each resource.

UNDERSTANDING GOD: A GREAT PLACE TO BEGIN

Understanding God is the book in The Discipling Cycle Series which guides the student in knowing God. Youth will be strengthened in personal disciplines and character qualities. This is an ideal place to begin the series. However, it is not necessary that you start The Discipling Cycle Series with any specific book in the series. It has not been developed with a "book one, book two, book three" approach. In fact, *Understanding God* could be book one, two, or three, depending on where a student begins the cycle. You can begin The Discipling Cycle Series with any of the three workbooks in the series. The Bible study leader will find many helpful suggestions to facilitate this program in the *Understanding God Leader's Guide* (ISBN 0-6330-3538-6), also available at LifeWay Christian Stores or by calling 1-800-458-2772.

SCRIPTURE MEMORY

Scripture memory is an important aspect of *Understanding God*, and a vital part of each week's journey. Without Scripture memory, a serious study of the Bible will be significantly impaired. As the believer memorizes the verses suggested in *Understanding God*, he or she will see how the Holy Spirit uses the verses to hold the believer accountable to principles learned each week. These verses will help form a clear image of what the believer's life is supposed to look like.

The weekly verses in *Understanding God* can be memorized by topic or title. Although the majority of Scripture memory topics are the same as the title of the study, some are different. Always use the topic found inside the Scripture Memory box on Day 1 of each study. Below is an example of how the verses will be listed each week.

SCRIPTURE MEMORY
Lordship of Christ
■ **Philippians 2:10-11**
■ **Colossians 1:17**
■ **2 Corinthians 5:14-15**

In most of the studies you will find three verses in the Scripture Memory box, but you only need to choose and memorize one of the verses each week. When you have selected your verse for the week, write it on a card or piece of paper and place it somewhere you spend a lot of time.

This is the way you will want to memorize: topic to reference; reference to verse. When someone helps you review your verses, ask him or her to give you the topic, then you recite the Scripture reference and quote the verse.

Make use of idle minutes by reviewing your verses. Take your verses with you to school and ask someone in your class, a nonbeliever maybe, to test you on them when you have free time. Scripture memory is a challenge, but it can also be fun. And you will never look back and regret having done it! Make this a serious commitment. You will soon see that the rewards are grand compared to the little time and effort it takes to memorize Scripture. Decide now to make Scripture memory a priority.

DAILY BIBLE STUDY

In addition to the Scripture Memory box, each week includes five days of Bible study relating to that week's topic. It is set up this way to encourage daily Bible study. You will gain much more from a study in The Discipling Cycle Series when you approach it daily, rather than doing it all at once. Thirty weeks is a long haul. Determine now to make this a priority not only for week 1, but for week 9, week 15, week 22, every week. And for those weeks when you fail, remember that you are not on a performance basis with God. It was not your works that saved you; it is not your works that keep you right before Him. Don't let guilt become your motivator, for it will not motivate. It will only tie you up in a noose. Learn to recognize the gentle prompting of the Holy Spirit. Don't work to please God, work because you already please God in Christ! Embrace this truth for yourself on the bad days as well as the good days.

The studies contain a variety of types of questions. Some will have obvious answers from the passage. Some will be personal and will require a more individual answer. Others will cause you to think and will not necessarily have one right answer. If you find that you do not understand a question, give the Holy Spirit some time to make it clear to you. It may be that you still do not receive an answer. Maybe He is not dealing with you in this particular area. If this happens, do not get discouraged, simply move on to the next question.

We are constantly amazed at the level of depth that students exhibit in answering questions in this study, and even more excited about how their actions reflect a true grasp of the principles. You have that same potential. Never let Satan convince you otherwise!

CONCEPT OF GOD SURVEY

There is much to learn about the character of God and your concept of who He is and what He is like. Complete the following survey on the basis of what you know and feel about God. Write down *the first thing that comes to your mind,* not what you think is the "right" answer. When you have completed this study you will complete an identical survey. You will observe how your concept of God changed.

Today's date _____

1. The first word that comes to my mind when I think about God is _____.

2. When I think about God, I feel _____.

3. If I do something I shouldn't have done, God will _____.

4. Sometimes I wish God would _____.

5. The thing I need to change to please God is _____.

6. The thing that frustrates me most about God is _____.

7. God surprises me when _____.

8. One thing I'm afraid God will do is _____.

9. I feel that God wants to take _____ away from me.

10. If God told me to do something I would feel _____.

11. God gives me something so that He _____.

12. I don't think God loves me when _____.

13. God helps me only when I _____.

14. God is farthest away from me when _____.

15. I don't feel God listens to me when I _____.

16. In times of need I don't turn to God because _____.

17. I feel that my problems are _____ for God.

18. I feel God always forgets _____.

19. It is hard for me to pray to God when/because _____.

20. If I made Christ the Lord of my life, then _____.

Concept of God test inspired by Michael Wells, *Sidetracked in the Wilderness* (Tarrytown: Revell, 1991) 58-59.

WEEK 1
THE LORDSHIP OF JESUS CHRIST

DAY 1

The word *Lord* simply means "master." Every person, Christian or not, submits to something as master of his or her life. It may be another person; it may be a set of philosophies. And then again it may be the person, himself. As a Christian, you may already be thinking, *Yes, but I have already determined that Jesus is the Lord of my life.* But *is* He really Lord? Is it enough to recognize His lordship with your lips? If He *is* Savior, does that automatically mean that He is lord? These are questions we will examine in this study. We will also see how Christ's lordship relates to all of creation.

Sanctify Christ as Lord in your hearts (1 Pet. 3:15).

Read Colossians 1:15-20.

1. **Verse 15—How do we know what God looks like, what His character is like, what His personality is like?**

2. **Verse 16—Check the things below which were created by Christ and for Him.**

    ❑ angels   ❑ Christians
    ❑ family   ❑ trees
    ❑ heaven   ❑ non-Christians
    ❑ music   ❑ governments

3. **Why were you created?**

4. **Verse 17—Why is it significant that Christ existed before anything else?**

5. **Do you know anyone whose life does not seem to be held together by Christ? How do you think verse 17 relates to him or her?**

SCRIPTURE MEMORY
Lordship of Christ
■ **Philippians 2:10-11**
■ **Colossians 1:17**
■ **2 Corinthians 5:14-15**

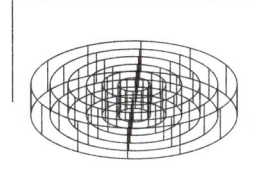

6. **Jesus is first. He is Lord and Creator. This is true whether any person recognizes Him as Lord or not. He is Lord of the universe and Lord of the church—the body of believers. How many Christians experience His Lordship in a way that the unsaved do not?**

7. **How many Christians experience His Lordship in these areas?**

   Sin

   Relationships

   The future

8. **As a believer you have the privilege of allowing the first-born of all creation to be Lord in every area of your life through the Holy Spirit who lives in you. A non-believer does not have the choice—he is lord of his own life until he allows Jesus to become Savior. What are the dangers of being lord of your own life?**

"In every Christian's heart there is a cross and a throne, and the Christian is on the throne till he puts himself on the cross; if he refuses the cross he remains on the throne. Perhaps this is at the bottom of the backsliding and worldliness among gospel believers today. We want to be saved but we insist that Christ do all the dying. No cross for us, no dethronement, no dying. We remain king."[1]

9. **How do you know that you are truly making Him Lord?**

10. **Look through Colossians 1:15-20 again and find three reasons why He is worthy to be the Lord of your life.**

    1.

    2.

    3.

DAY 2

Yesterday's study ended with Christ's *worthiness* to be Lord—the Master of a person's life. Today we will look at one of the things that rivals Him most for control—people.

Read Psalm 146:1-10.

11. **Verse 2—How do you think a Christian who has submitted to the lordship of Christ will praise Him in ways other than words?**

12. How does a person reveal who his lord is by how he acts?

13. List four reasons why any one person is not worthy of being the lord of your life. (vv. 3-4)

    1.

    2.

    3.

    4.

14. Think of the person whose opinions matter most to you (it may be yourself), then answer yes or no to the following:

    Can that person save you from sin and hell? ❑ yes ❑ no
    Will that person die someday? ❑ yes ❑ no
    Do they possess all knowledge? ❑ yes ❑ no
    Can they see into the future? ❑ yes ❑ no

15. Verse 5—Why is a person blessed if he trusts these and other issues to God?

16. List the objects or people that God watches over. (vv. 6-9)

17. Is there anyone who is not under His watch?

18. Verse 10—When every person whom you know "returns to the earth," what will the Lord be doing?

19. List three reasons from Psalm 146:1-10 why Christ is worthy to be Lord and why His opinions should matter most.

    1.

    2.

    3.

DAY 3

One of the things that will distinguish a person who is making Jesus the Lord of his life is that he will live by a set of standards that is different from the world's standards. Today, we will see why a person cannot follow both.

Read 1 John 2:15-17.

20. Why is it impossible to love both the Father and the world?

The World Says	God Says
Become rich.	Do not weary yourself to gain wealth, Cease from your consideration of it (Prov. 23:4).
Make a name for yourself.	Humble yourselves, therefore, under the mighty hand of God, that He may exalt you at the proper time (1 Pet. 5:6).
Disown people who have hurt you Hurt them back.	"I say to you, love your enemies, and pray for those who persecute you" (Matt. 5:44).
Live your life according to what you think is best.	Therefore be imitators of God, as beloved children (Eph. 5:1).
Look out for number one. No one else is going to.	Do not merely look out for your own personal interests, but also for the interests of others (Phil. 2:4).
It's okay to have premarital sex if you really love the person.	Let marriage be held in honor among all, and let the marriage bed be undefiled; for fornicators and adulterers God will judge (Heb. 13:4).
Please your teacher, coach, boss, friend. They can help you get ahead.	Am I now seeking the favor of men, or of God? Or am I striving to please men? If I were still trying to please men, I would not be a bond-servant of Christ" (Gal. 1:10).
Don't listen to your parents; they're so old-fashioned.	Children, obey your parents in the Lord, for this is right (Eph. 6:1).

It's clear. What the Father commands for your life and what the world suggests rarely (if ever) agree. It really is impossible to please both.

Jesus said in Matthew 6:24, "No one can serve two masters; for either he will hate the one and love the other, or he will hold to one and despise the other. You cannot serve both God and mammon."

21. How will a person who grows in his love for the things of the world, lessen in his affection for God?

22. Likewise, how will a person who increases in his love for Christ lessen in his affection for the world?

23. Verse 16—Satan tempts us the same way he did Christ in the garden (Matt. 4), through the lust of the eye, the lust of the flesh, and the boastful pride of life. Can you think of an example of each?

Lust of the eye.

Lust of the flesh.

Boastful pride of life.

24. Verse 17—Why are the claims of the world not worthy of giving your life?

25. Why is God's instruction worthy of us living by?

DAY 4

In today's study we will discover the difference between Jesus' lordship of all creation and His lordship in the individual life of the believer. We will also continue to deepen the conviction that He alone is worthy to be Master.

Read Philippians 2:5-11.

26. Verse 5—Making Jesus Lord is not limited to our words and actions. He can also be Lord of our attitudes. Name one attitude in your life that would not be found in Jesus.

27. Circle the qualities you are likely to find in someone who is making Jesus Lord. (vv. 6-8)

Humility	Mercy
Boastfulness	Self-exaltation
Self-denial	Obedience to self
Servanthood	Exclusion of others
Obedience to God	

28. What happened to Jesus when He humbled Himself?

29. What happens when we humble ourselves?

30. Notice the words that characterize the Lord of lords in this passage: "emptied," "humbled," "servant." What words does the world's value system use to characterize a person on his way to the "top"?

31. Was Jesus forced to be obedient? Are we forced to make Him Lord?

32. Verse 10—Does it say that every tongue will confess Jesus as *Savior?* How will they acknowledge Him?

33. Does everyone who has made Jesus his Savior automatically make Him his Lord? Explain.

34. When does Jesus become Lord?

35. Look through Philippians 2:5-11 again and list three reasons why Jesus is worthy to be the Lord of your life.

   1.

   2.

   3.

Today's study will help you determine if you are making Jesus the Lord of your own life and how His lordship is lived out moment by moment.

Read 2 Corinthians 5:14-15.

36. Verse 14—What does this verse say should be the motivation for making Jesus Lord of our lives?

Do you love Jesus more than anything or anyone else? If no, do you desire to? Ask Him to give you a new and stronger love for Him.

37. Verse 15—How do you know when you are loving Jesus more than anything or anyone else according to this verse?

38. Reflect on the following questions. You may want to record answers in the margin.

   Should I live my life for Christ, myself, or another person?

   Should I place my security/identity in myself, my looks, my talents, what others think of me, or in Christ?

Should I place my significance or worth as a person in Christ alone?

Should I base my decisions on what Christ desires, on what others think, or on what I want to do?

"Whatever controls us really is our god. ... The person who seeks power is controlled by power. The person who seeks acceptance is controlled by the people he or she wants to please. We do not control ourselves. We are controlled by the lord of our life."[3]

39. What risks do you take in letting Christ have control of your life?

40. What risks do you take if you are in control of your life?

"Jesus owns his people. He is not a despot or tyrant, as we might expect in an earthly slave/master situation. In fact, the irony of New Testament lordship is the irony that only in slavery to Christ can a man discover authentic freedom. The irony is pushed further by the New Testament teaching that it is through a slave/master relationship to Jesus that a person is liberated from bondage in this world."[4]

A "lordship decision" is a decision which is based upon what Jesus would do in a particular situation. It is a decision that is not merely of the mind, but of the will. It is a decision of action. In determining to make Jesus the Lord of one's life, it is not a "one-time" decision. It is not even a daily decision. It is a moment by moment decision. Choosing to make Jesus the Lord in one decision does not mean that He will be made the Lord of the next decision. In fact, the person who is truly making Jesus the Lord of His life will find himself asking the question several times a day, "What would Jesus do in this situation?"

> "If we want to be disciples, we place ourselves, like the football player and the instrumentalist, under someone's direction. He tells us what to do, and we find our happiness in doing it. We will not find it anywhere else. We will not find it by doing only what we want to do and not doing what we don't want to do. That is the popular idea of what freedom is, but it does not work. Freedom lies in keeping the rules."[5]
> —Elisabeth Elliot

[1]A. W. Tozer, *The Root of the Righteous* (Camp Hill: Christian Publications, 1955, 1986), 66.
[2]Rebecca Manley Pippert, *Out of the Salt Shaker & into the World* (Downers Grove: InterVarsity Press, 1979), 43.
[3]Pippert, *Out of the Salt Shaker & into the World*, 52.
[4]R. C. Sproul, *Who Is Jesus?* (Orlando: Ligonier Ministries, 1999), 32.
[5]Elisabeth Elliot, *Discipline: The Glad Surrender* (Old Tappan: Fleming H. Revell, a division of Baker Book House Company, 1982), 37.

WEEK 2
FELLOWSHIP WITH GOD

SCRIPTURE MEMORY
Fellowship with God
- Psalm 63:1
- Mark 1:35
- Philippians 3:10

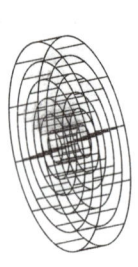

DAY 1

God created man to have fellowship with Him. When that fellowship was broken because of sin, God sent His Son so that the relationship could be restored. The purpose of sending Jesus was not so that He could merely "introduce" us to the Father, but that we might enjoy an intimate, daily, abiding fellowship with Him—so that we might *know* Him. Unfortunately, there are many hindrances in our schedules. Christians often find that this greatest privilege of fellowshipping with God is also our greatest point of defeat. Today we will look at the emphasis Jesus, Himself, placed upon His time alone with the Father, how He handled the obstacles, and how His example impacts us.

Read Mark 1:32-38.

1. **Many people requested Jesus' attention. What type of people are mentioned in verses 32-34,36?**

2. **Verse 33—What pressures have gathered at the "door" of your life?**

3. **Why do you think Jesus can relate? (vv. 32-34)**

4. **When do you think the pressures will quit banging on your "door"?**

5. **Verse 35—What did Jesus make a special effort to do?**

6. **What example does this set for you?**

7. **Which would be best for you? (check one)**

   ❏ Wait for a free moment to spend time alone with God.
   ❏ Decide on a pre-planned time.

8. If the whole "city" were at your door, how would it impact your time with God?

9. Why do you think Jesus set aside time alone to pray when there were so many needs to be met?

10. Verse 38—Jesus felt led to the "towns nearby." He would probably find the same needs in these towns that He found in the one in which He was staying. How did He know He was supposed to go?

DAY 2

Every relationship is twofold. Of course, some relationships reach a deeper level than others. More than any other, your relationship with the Lord is the one in which you should experience the most intimacy. God has accomplished everything to make that possible. Meeting with Him on a daily basis is a response to something He has already initiated with you.

11. What are some specific things you can do to respond to Him daily, according to the following verses?

Psalm 61:1

Psalm 62:1

Psalm 63:1

Psalm 64:1

Psalm 65:1

Psalm 66:1

Psalm 67:1

12. Which of the above is the most difficult for you to give to your relationship with God? Why?

Acknowledge this weakness to the Lord now and give it to Him.

13. Look again at Psalm 62:1. Which of the following does the psalmist wait for in this verse?

❑ The Lord's blessings
❑ Removal of stress
❑ God Himself
❑ Guidance for the future

"Good things as well as bad, you know, are caught by a kind of infection. If you want to get warm you must stand near the fire: if you want to be wet you must get into the water. If you want joy, power, peace, eternal life, you must get close to, or even into, the thing that has them . . . If you are close to it, the spray will wet you: if you are not you will remain dry."[1]
—C. S. Lewis

14. Look again at Psalm 63:1. Which of the following does the psalmist yearn for?

   ❑ The Lord's blessings
   ❑ Removal of stress
   ❑ Guidance for the future
   ❑ God Himself

15. What difference do you see between your attitude and the psalmist's attitude in meeting with the Lord?

That I may know Him, and the power of His resurrection and the fellowship of His sufferings, being conformed to His death (Phil. 3:10).

The vow will be performed (Ps. 65:1).

16. What is a recent vow you have made to the Lord in which you have not followed through?

17. What impact would daily time with the Lord have upon this promise (or vow) and others?

18. The verses you have read are genuine prayers written many centuries ago. Hopefully their honesty has encouraged you in your relationship with God. If you could write a word of encouragement to be read by someone a hundred years from now about their relationship with God, what would you write?

"Our spiritual forefathers . . . determined to have 'hearts for God' . . . That is why their diaries would sometimes contain *vows,* or *covenants* they would make to the Lord. In His presence they would commit themselves, by His grace, to remember Him and to live the whole of their lives before Him."[3]

Most often it is not a negative thing that we allow to thwart our time alone with God; sometimes it is a good thing—a very "spiritual" thing. In fact it is often the very ministry we've committed ourselves to that becomes our greatest hindrance to meeting with God. This was the case for Martha as we shall see in today's study.

Read Luke 10:38-42.

19. Answer each question on the next page with one of the following three responses: "Martha," "Mary," or "both."

Who was in the presence of Jesus?

Who put more emphasis on service than on Jesus?

Who had her eyes on what others were doing rather than on Jesus?

Who had the most intimate time with Jesus?

Whose eyes were focused on the eternal?

Who knew Jesus best?

To an occupant of the house who would seem to be more spiritual?

Who did not give in to the pressures around her?

Whom do you relate to the most?

20. **In your life, what most competes with Jesus for your time?**

21. **Why is it our tendency to allow such things to come before Christ?**

Reflecting upon today's passage, Luke 10:38-42, Ken Gire writes, "He brings his point gently home: Fellowship with him is a matter of priorities. And a matter of choice. It's the better part of the meal life has to offer. It is, in fact, the main course."[4]

22. **Have you ever compared your walk with God to someone else's? Why does God want a unique relationship with you?**

23. **Martha could easily have talked to Jesus while she was preparing dinner. (She did. See v. 40.) In the same way we can talk to Jesus while we are accomplishing our tasks. We should! His presence never leaves us. But why do you think it's important to spend time with Jesus the way Mary did?**

Ken Gire also prays, "Guard my heart this day from the many distractions that vie for my attention. And help me to fix my eyes on you. Not on my rank in the kingdom, as did the disciples. Not on the finer points of theology, as did the scribes. Not on the sins of others as did the Pharisees. Not on a place of worship, as did the woman at the well. Not on the budget, as did Judas. But on you."[5]

Could this become your prayer today, too?

DAY 4

The more time we spend in fellowship with another person, the more likely we are to recognize the sound of his or her voice. The same is true of God. Casual contact with Jesus is not enough. If time alone with God is not a priority, we fall prey to the deceiver who will try to make us think that his voice is really the Shepherd's voice. And if we're not spending time learning to recognize the voice of God, then we will start listening to and believing in the voice of the enemy.

Read John 10:1-15.

24. **If the sheep are Christians, who should we be listening to? (vv. 3-5)**

25. **Why do you think some Christians always listen to Jesus' voice?**

26. **How can you distinguish the voice of Jesus from all the other voices you hear?**

27. **Read each statement. Next to each circle T for "thief" or S for "shepherd" to indicate which voice would say the statement.**

    T S You are acceptable to me and I love you.

    T S You must work to please God because you will fail Him, and He will be displeased with you.

    T S Work for God's favor.

    T S You already have God's favor.

    T S If you don't spend time with God today, He will be disappointed in you.

    T S Spend time with God because you love Him and because He loves you.

    T S Don't allow yourself to be put in a vulnerable position where you might be tempted to sin.

    T S You are a strong Christian; you would never give in to temptation.

    T S You're doing okay in your Christian walk. You may not be the best Christian, but you're certainly not the worst.

    T S Don't work for God to gain His approval; work because you already are perfect in His eyes.

28. **Place each word or phrase under the heading that would most likely be the source of the words.**

hurtful	gentle	loving	leading
harsh	critical	teaching	lifts my spirit
condemning	depressing	confusing	brings life
	driving	brings freedom	

   Shepherd   **Thief**

29. **Answer "yes," "no," or "sometimes" to the following questions:**

   Have you ever had trouble distinguishing these two voices?
   Do you listen and follow the Shepherd's voice?
   Do you listen and follow the thief's voice?

Right before Jesus' crucifixion He prayed a prayer for the 12 men He had discipled. It is recorded in the Gospel of John.

"Sanctify them in the truth; Thy word is truth" (John. 17:17).

30. **What source will always help you distinguish the Shepherd's voice?**

31. **Think about five people whose voices you would recognize on the telephone before they even told you their name. Why would you recognize their voices?**

32. **What does this indicate to you about recognizing the voice of Jesus?**

33. **Who knows you intimately? (See John 10:14-15.)**

34. **Circle the number which you feel would represent the level of intimacy that you experience with God. (5 being very intimate)**

             1   2   3   4   5

"The Christian who is satisfied to give God His 'minute' and to have 'a little talk with Jesus' is the same one who shows up at the evangelistic service weeping over his retarded spiritual growth and begging the evangelist to show him the way out of his difficulty."[6]

Pray that God would give you a heart to intimately know Him and ears to clearly recognize His voice.

DAY 5

Advertising experts use many tactics to get our attention. They'll shock us, scream at us, manipulate our emotions, or do whatever it takes to fix their product in our minds. These things work. God also can (and does) use big events in our lives to get our attention. We turn to God in tragedy, depression, defeat. How do we respond to the big events or circumstances in our lives when time alone with God is a regular part of our lives? Think about it.

35. **If you witnessed a tornado, an earthquake, and a massive fire all in the same day what would you think?**

Read 1 Kings 19:9-14.

36. **What were Elijah's circumstances? (v. 10)**

37. Elijah felt defeated, lonely, opposed, and threatened. When have you felt like Elijah?

38. Where had Elijah's circumstances led him? (v. 9)

39. Where was the Lord not to be found? (vv. 11-12)

40. Where does Scripture indicate that the Lord was?

41. How can you relate your own personal time of fellowship with the Lord to Elijah's experience?

Walk into an arcade and notice the competition between video games. Each game seems to try to out do the other with brighter lights and louder bells.

Listen to a commercial and you might hear an announcer yell at you to buy something.

The Lord does not play games with you to get your attention. He has nothing to sell. He is who He was. Creator, Savior, Lifegiver. He is God and He is worthy of our time.

[1]*Mere Christianity* by C. S. Lewis, copyright © C. S. Lewis Pte. Ltd. 1942, 1943, 1944, 1952. Extract reprinted by permission, 137.

[2]*Lord of the Impossible*, Lloyd John Ogilvie, 1984, Abingdon Press, 83. Used by permission.

[3]*A Heart for God*, Sinclair B. Ferguson, © 1985,164. Used by Permission of NavPress/Pinon Press.All rights reserved. For Copies call 1-800-366-7788.

[4]Ken Gire, *Intimate Moments With the Savior* (Grand Rapids: Zondervan, 1989), 67.

[5]Ibid, 69.

[6]A. W. Tozer, *The Root of the Righteous* (Camp Hill: Christian Publications, 1955, 1986), 12.

WEEK 3
THE HOLY SPIRIT

DAY 1

SCRIPTURE MEMORY
The Holy Spirit
■ **John 16:13**
■ **Romans 8:11**
■ **Galatians 5:22-23**

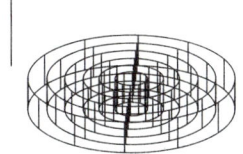

Many people have tried to explain the three-person Godhead known as the Trinity. The subject is complex with certain aspects of mystery. But the subject is not one we can ignore simply because we do not comprehend it all. We may not understand everything about digestion, but that doesn't keep us from enjoying a good steak now and then. The Trinity is echoed throughout Scripture, from beginning to end. One God in three Persons is described in Scripture:

The Father is God *invisible*—John 1:18
The Son is God *revealed*—John 1:14; Hebrews 1:1-4
The Holy Spirit is God *working in men*—John 16:8; 1 Corinthians 2:10

C. S. Lewis writes, "An ordinary simple Christian kneels down to say his prayers. He is trying to get into touch with God. But if he is a Christian he knows that what is prompting him to pray is also God: God, so to speak, inside him. But he also knows that all his real knowledge of God comes through Christ, the Man who was God—that Christ is standing beside him, helping him to pray, praying for him. You see what is happening. God is the thing to which he is praying—the goal he is trying to reach. God is also the thing inside him which is pushing him on—the motive power. God is also the road or bridge along which he is being pushed to that goal. So that the whole threefold life of the three-personal Being is actually going on in that ordinary little bedroom where an ordinary man is saying his prayers."[1]

The Holy Spirit is one with the Father and one with the Son in the Godhead. The following verses show us His deity, His equality with God.

He is eternal—Hebrews 9:14
He is all powerful—Luke 1:35
He is present everywhere—Psalm 139:7
He is all-knowing—1 Corinthians 2:10-11
He is Creator—Colossians 1:16-17

He is also a person. Jesus never refers to the Holy Spirit as "it." He speaks of Him as "He." The following verses reveal His personhood in three categories.

Intellect
He speaks (Acts 13:2)
He intercedes (Rom. 8:26)
He testifies (Rom. 8:26)

Sensibility
He can be lied to (Acts 5:3-4)
He can be insulted (Heb. 10:29)
He can be grieved (Eph. 4:30)

Will
He distributes spiritual gifts as He desires (1 Cor. 12:11)
He leads (Acts 8:29)
He commands (Acts 16:6-7)
He guides (John 16:13)
He appoints (Acts 20:28)

A. W. Tozer writes, "The Persons of the Godhead never work separately. We dare not think of them in such a way as to 'divide the substance.' Every act of God is done by all three Persons. God is never anywhere present in one Person without the other two. He cannot divide Himself. Where the Spirit is, there also is the Father and the Son ... For the accomplishment of some specific work one Person may for the time be more prominent than the others are, but never is He alone. God is altogether present wherever He is present at all."[2]

Read John 15:26-27 and 16:7-15.

1. Verse 26—Who sent the Holy Spirit?

2. From where was He sent?

3. What is the purpose of the Holy Spirit in relation to the following?

Non-believers (John 16:8-10)

Believers (John 16:10,13)

Satan (John 16:11)

Jesus (John 16:14)

Though the Holy Spirit acts as a defense attorney in behalf of the believer, He is the prosecutor to the non-believer. The word *convict* in verse 8 means to cross examine with the purpose of convincing or refuting an opponent.

The Holy Spirit reveals to the nonbeliever the truth about *sin, righteousness,* and *judgment.* The people in Jesus' day thought that He was a sinner and that they were righteous. The Holy Spirit reveals what *sin* is—unbelief (vv. 8-9). This is the basic sin by which every sin comes. It is rebellion. It says, "I will not believe in Jesus." The Holy Spirit reveals to the nonbeliever that *righteousness* is completely dependent upon Jesus' atonement (v. 10). In regard to *judgment* He reveals to the sinner that Satan, the prince of the world (and in essence the "prince" of their life) has been judged already at the cross.

Jesus answered, "No one can come to Me, unless the Father who sent Me draws him; and I will raise him up on the last day" (John 6:44). God, through the Holy Spirit, initiates a relationship with the unbeliever. The idea to come to the Father through Jesus never originates in the heart of any person. It is only when the Holy Spirit moves in the unbeliever's heart in regard to their sin and the atoning work of Christ that a person may come to know God.

When the Holy Spirit has been able to do His work in the believer and in His church, He then has the freedom to do His work in the unbeliever.

"He will guide you" (v. 13.)

4. What does the term *guide* reveal to you about the Holy Spirit? (Think of *guide* in contrast to the words control, force, or drive.)

"Into all truth" (v. 13.)

5. Why can you turn to the Holy Spirit in times of decision-making?

"He will not speak on His own initiative." (v. 13.)

6. How has God used the Holy Spirit as His Messenger in your life?

DAY 2

Read Ephesians 3:14-19.

7. Where is the Holy Spirit's power fulfilled in the life of the believer according to verse 16?

8. How is this different from the world's concept of power?

9. Look at these words from verses 17,18,19. *Dwell, rooted, grounded, comprehend, know, filled.* What do you see as the Holy Spirit's work when you consider these words in light of the passage?

10. Verse 19 says, "to know the love of Christ which surpasses knowledge." Why would this statement seem to contradict itself to someone who does not possess the Holy Spirit?

"Jesus wanted His disciples, and us, to come to know God, in all the riches and fullness of His being. He wanted us to know God in His eternal glory and to recognize how great He is; but He also wanted us to see that the God whose being we cannot comprehend is also the God who is a Father who loves us, a Son who came to die for us, a Spirit who brings us into God's heart and who brings God into our hearts."[3]
—Sinclair B. Ferguson

> "The Holy Spirit is the One Who makes real in you all that Jesus did for you."[4]
> —Oswald Chambers

To us God revealed them through the Spirit; for the Spirit searches all things, even the depths of God. For who among men knows the thoughts of a man except the spirit of the man, which is in him? Even so the thoughts of God no one knows except the Spirit of God (1 Cor. 2:10-11).

DAY 3

The Holy Spirit is literally Christ's life *in* you. Today we will discover some of the specifics that the Holy Spirit is able to accomplish in you, while contrasting the inadequacy of the flesh's ability to do what God commands.

Read Romans 8:1-27.

11. **As you read through today's passage, find the verse(s) that coincides with the ministries of the Holy Spirit listed below and write the reference next to it.**

    He gives power to overcome sin.
    He assures us of our salvation.
    He has set us free.
    He gives life and peace.
    He searches our hearts.
    He gives us power to walk in the Spirit.
    He lives inside of us.
    He has given us adoption as sons and the rights of an heir.
    He has been given to us through Christ.
    He raised Jesus from the dead.
    He prays for us.
    He knows the will of God.
    He takes away fear.

The Holy Spirit has brought Jesus into your life to empower you to do everything the Father commands you to do.

He says, "My grace is sufficient for you, for power is perfected in weakness" (2 Cor. 12:9). Do you have a person in your life who is hard to love? The Holy Spirit can love them through you.

Do you have a sin that is hard to overcome? The Holy Spirit can overcome this in you. "Greater is He who is in you than he who is in the world" (1 John 4:4). It is only when we admit that we are incapable of pleasing God in our own strength that the Holy Spirit's power is perfected in us.

12. **What do the following verses say about the "body" or the "flesh?"**

    Verse 6

    Verse 7

    Verse 8

Verse 10

Verse 13

13. What do the following verses say about the "Spirit"?

Verse 6

Verse 10

Verse 13

Verse 14

14. Verse 11—What did the Holy Spirit accomplish?

15. Where is He today according to this verse?

16. How does this encourage you in areas where you experience defeat?

In the same way the Spirit also helps our weaknesses (v. 26).

17. Name an area in your life in which it is hard to admit you are weak.

Do you know what can happen even now with this weak area, according to verse 26? Give it up. Your flesh isn't qualified to accomplish it. Spend time with the Lord in prayer over this area.

DAY 4

Sometimes the terminology we use to explain Christian doctrine is confusing. This is especially true in the doctrine of the Holy Spirit. Let's address two of the most common questions related to the Holy Spirit.

What does it mean to be baptized in the Spirit?

A person is baptized by the Holy Spirit one time—at the time of conversion.

By one Spirit we were all baptized into one body, whether Jews or Greeks, whether slaves or free, and we were all made to drink of one Spirit (1 Cor. 12:13).

> "The Holy Spirit is God's answer to the problem of righteous living. He is the abiding presence of Christ's life in you."[5]
> —Charles Stanley

> "The Spirit-filled (or Spirit-controlled) life begins with an overwhelming realization that we are absolutely helpless and hopeless apart from the empowerment of the Holy Spirit. Until that one simple truth grips us at the core of our being, we will never experience the full-blown power of the Holy Spirit."[6]
> —Charles Stanley

One Lord, one faith, one baptism (Eph. 4:5).

Peter told the people to repent and be baptized in the name of Christ for the forgiveness of their sins. Then they would receive the gift of the Holy Spirit (Acts 2:38-39). What does it mean to be filled with the Holy Spirit?

When you received Christ into your heart, you received all of the Holy Spirit—He baptized you with Christ's Spirit. But being *filled* with the Holy Spirit deals more with the question, "Does the Holy Spirit have all of me?" It comes down to control—Spirit-filled is Spirit-controlled.

Do not get drunk with wine, for that is dissipation, but be filled with the Spirit (Eph. 5:18).

Read Ephesians 5:18-21.

18. **When a person is drunk, how does alcohol the affect the following?**

    abilities

    personality

    actions

    words

    thoughts

19. **When a person is filled with the Spirit, how will the following be affected?**

    abilities

    personality

    actions

    words

    thoughts

20. **Match the following expressions of being filled with the Spirit with the corresponding verse.**

    ___ Verse 19   A. Accommodation
    ___ Verse 20   B. Adoration
    ___ Verse 21   C. Appreciation

21. **Write your week 1 memory verse ("Lordship of Christ").**

22. How is being filled with the Spirit related to surrendering to Christ's Lordship of your life?

DAY 5

Today's lesson characterizes the Spirit-filled life while exposing the life that is controlled by the flesh. What may *look* like a Spirit-filled life may not necessarily be one. The real test is not so much what is on the outside, but the *Source* of what is produced on the outside.

Read Galatians 5:16-24.

23. **Verses 19-23 describe a person who is controlled by the Spirit and one who walks in the flesh. Look up the definitions of any words you do not understand. Write definitions in the space below.**

24. **What is one deed with which you struggle?**

25. **How can you overcome this struggle? (v. 16)**

26. **Verse 17—As Christians, we face the inward struggle between the flesh and the Spirit. Describe a situation when your flesh wanted one thing and your Spirit wanted the opposite.**

27. **At first glance the deeds of the flesh may promise some appealing things—temporary thrills, fun, acceptance. But what is one thing the deeds of the flesh cannot promise? (v. 21)**

28. **Artificial fruit can be mistaken for the real thing, but if it didn't grow on a tree, it's not real. Likewise, you may notice non-Christians demonstrating what looks like the fruit of the Spirit (Gal. 5:22-23), but on closer examination is not the real thing. How do you distinguish the artificial from the authentic even in your own life?**

29. **Verse 25—What do you think it means to "walk by the Spirit?"**

"People who are always looking for a way to direct or control the power of the Holy Spirit are confused. *The Holy Spirit was sent to control us!* He is not available to do our bidding. He is looking for surrendered believers to do His."[7]
—Charles Stanley

[1]*Mere Christianity* by C. S. Lewis copyright © C. S. Lewis Pte. Ltd. 1942, 1943, 1944, 1952, 127. Extract reprinted by permission.
[2]A. W. Tozer, *The Divine Conquest* (Harrisburg: Christian Publications, Inc., 1950), 73.
[3]*A Heart for God*, Sinclair B. Ferguson, © 1985, 40. Used by Permission of NavPress/Pinon Press. All rights reserved. For Copies call 1-800-366-7788.
[4]Oswald Chambers, *My Utmost for His Highest* (Westwood: Barbour and Company, Inc., 1935, 1963), 117.
[5]Charles Stanley, *The Wonderful Spirit Filled Life* (Nashville: Thomas Nelson, 1992), 65.
[6]Ibid, 47.
[7]Ibid, 114.

WEEK 4
THE ABIDING LIFE

SCRIPTURE MEMORY
Abiding in Christ
■ John 15:5

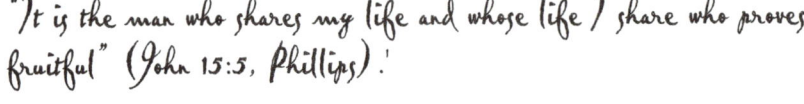

"It is the man who shares my life and whose life I share who proves fruitful" (John 15:5, Phillips).[1]

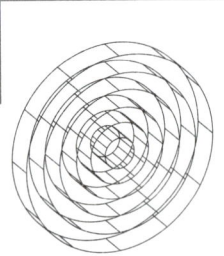

DAY 1

Read Genesis 2:8-9,15-17 and Genesis 3:1-24. Adam and Eve ate from the tree of the knowledge of good and evil. One question to think about.

1. Adam and Eve had no knowledge of evil before they ate the fruit. But apparently they had no knowledge of good either. With no knowledge of good or evil, how would you describe the deeds they performed before they ate from the tree?

DAY 2

Read Psalm 1:1-6.

The psalmist compares a person and a tree. As we will see through Scripture, trees have a lot to teach us about our spiritual lives.

2. A healthy tree must be planted in good soil. Likewise, for a Christian to thrive in his spiritual life he must be planted in rich "soil." What does not make up the right soil according to verse 1?

3. A healthy tree must also have nourishment. How does verse 2 describe the spiritual nourishment of a fruitful Christian?

"One swallow does not make a spring nor one hot day a summer; nor will a few minutes of frantic praying before service bring out the tender buds or make the flowers to appear on the earth. The field must be soaked in sunshine over a long period before it will give forth its treasures. The Christian's heart must be soaked in prayer before the true spiritual fruits begin to grow. As the field has learned to live intimately and sympathetically with the rain and the sunshine, so must the Christian learn to live with God. We cannot in a brief time make up for the long neglect of God and things spiritual."[2]

4. What do the words *delight* and *meditate* indicate is the fruitful Christian's attitude toward God's Word?

5. If you find a tree with good fruit you can be certain that it has a healthy root system. What you see on the branches only comes about as a result of what is taking place underground. How does this relate to the hidden life of the Christian?

6. Chaff is what is left over after the farmer harvests the wheat. It is worthless. In verse 4 the psalmist compares the wicked to chaff. How is chaff different from the tree described in verse 3?

7. How can you make the "soil" of your spiritual life richer?

8. How can you improve the nutritional intake in your spiritual life?

9. How can you help enrich the "soil" around you so that other Christians may become fruitful?

DAY 3

Read Jeremiah 17:5-8.

10. How does the tree in verse 6 respond to a desert situation?

11. How does the tree in verse 8 respond to a desert situation?

12. Why is the tree in verse 8 so fruitful?

13. How should your life parallel the tree in verse 8 in light of what you just wrote?

There are times when "the heat will come." We may face "a year of drought." Remember a time when you were fearful or anxious over a situation. You may have thought, *Maybe if I just prayed more things would be different.* Or, *If I was just more faithful in daily Bible study I would have a tighter grip on my circumstances.* But Jeremiah says, "It is the man who trusts in the Lord and whose trust is the Lord who will be like a tree firmly planted by the water." He did not say that it is the man who prays constantly, or it's the man who reads his Bible everyday.

In what are you placing your trust? It is easy sometimes to make prayer, Bible study, witnessing, and so forth the objects of our faith. But these should only be expressions of our trust in Him.

14. What does the stream represent in verse 8?

15. God has set up a "Trust" for you—Himself (v. 7). Name specific situations or needs in which you could depend upon this Trust.

16. What are other options in which you could place your trust? (v. 5)

17. What happens to the heart that trusts in these things? (v. 5)

18. Why does it seem easier sometimes to trust in the flesh (v. 5) rather than in God (v. 7)?

DAY 4

Jesus used trees to help distinguish between true and false teachers. The life of the teacher is the key. It is not what a person says or teaches but rather it is *what the teacher lives* that is passed on to his or her disciple.

19. If you were trying to identify an apple tree in an orchard what would you look for?

Read Matthew 7:15-20.

Society communicates a popular notion that what is right for one person may not be right for another. In the world's eyes, opened-mindedness is the greatest virtue. Truth is relative to the individual and his or her circumstances. Many Christians follow the theory that there is no black or white, no right or wrong. Everything falls into a gray area.

20. Why should you guard against broadening your own horizons with such philosophies? (v. 15)

21. Some trees do not originate from seeds but are off shoots of other trees. The off-shoot resembles the parent tree. When you think of yourself as becoming an "off shoot" of another person's teaching why should you be careful about from whom you will learn?

22. Why do you think Jesus emphasizes the life of a teacher rather than the words of a teacher?

23. "Who come to you in sheep's clothing"—If you were a non-Christian what would you do to make believers think you were one of them?

24. Why does Jesus point to the fruit in a person's life as the final test of what the person really is?

25. Jesus said in Matthew 7:1, "Do not judge lest you be judged." How can you distinguish the fruit in someone's life without judging him?

"A good tree cannot produce bad fruit" (Matt. 7:18b).

26. A good tree may occasionally produce a bad piece of fruit and a bad tree may occasionally produce a good piece of fruit. But these are the exceptions rather than the rule. How can you relate this to the lifestyles of believers and nonbelievers?

DAY 5

True success as a Christian is not what we are able to accomplish for God, but rather what *He* is able to accomplish in and through us. True success on God's terms is determined in how much of *Christ's life* we share in whatever we do. This is the abiding life.

27. What is the difference between the end result of a flower that is cut at the stem and put into a vase of water and one that is left uncut?

28. What happens to a branch that is removed from a tree and why?

Read John 15:1-8.

29. Who is the Vine in this illustration? (v. 1)

30. How does the Lord "prune" you?

"As the branch cannot bear fruit of itself, unless it abides in the vine" (John 15:4b).

Are you so foolish? Having begun by the Spirit, are you now being perfected by the flesh? (Gal. 3:3).

31. As Christians, we have very little trouble understanding that we are not saved by our works, that salvation is a free gift from God through Jesus Christ. But our actions after we are saved say that it's up to us to finish the process. Paul said this was foolish (Gal. 3:3). We try to "work up" the fruit we know we are supposed to possess as Christians. We try to do all the right things apart from Christ. What is the problem with this according to John 15:5?

> "The bough that breaks off from the tree in a storm may bloom briefly and give to the unthinking passer-by the impression that it is a healthy and fruitful branch, but its tender blossoms will soon perish and the bough itself wither and die. There is no lasting life apart from the root."[3]
> —A. W. Tozer

> **"Branches were not designed to produce fruit—they were designed to have fruit produced through them."[4]**
> —Charles Stanley

So what is fruit?

Jim Downing writes, "It is the overflow, the surplus, the excess life of the nourishment taken into the tree over and beyond that needed for life and growth. Fruit is simply *excess life.* Next time you hold an orange or an apple in your hand you can say, 'This is *excess life* which overflowed after the tree's need for nourishment and growth had been met.' "

"Many of us have seen the pathetic sight of a Christian trying to bear fruit. He has been trying through self-effort to work up courage to witness or be consistent in prayer. When we have partaken of the life of Christ in such abundance that our life-sustaining needs are met and our growth needs are met, the overflow of the love of Christ, the life of Christ, turns into fruit."[5]

J. B. Phillips translates John 15:4-5 like this, "You must go on growing in me and I will grow in you. For just as the branch cannot bear any fruit unless it shares the life of the vine, so you can produce nothing unless you go on growing in me. I am the vine itself, you are the branches. It is the man who shares my life and whose life I share who proves fruitful. For apart from me you can do nothing at all."[6]

32. There it is, the secret to what the Christian life is all about. What do you think it means to share in Christ's life?

33. What are the benefits of the abiding life? (v. 7)

"If you do not learn to abide in Christ, you will never have a marriage characterized by love, joy, and peace. You will never have the self-control necessary to consistently overcome temptation. And you will always be an emotional hostage of your circumstances."[7]

34. What is the motive of the abiding life? (v. 8)

Andrew Murray writes a beautiful prayer from the perspective of the abiding life. "Thou sayest: *Abide in me!* O my Master, my Life, my All, I do abide in Thee. Give Thou me to grow up into all Thy fullness. It is not the effort of faith, seeking to cling to Thee, nor even the rest of faith, trusting Thee to keep me; it is not the obedience of the will, nor the keeping of the commandments; but it is Thyself living in me as in the Father, that alone can satisfy me. It is Thyself, my Lord, no longer before me and above me, but one with me, and abiding in me; it is this I need, it is this I seek. It is this I trust Thee for."[8]

[1]Reprinted with permission of Macmillan Publishing Co., Inc. from J. B. Phillips: *The New Testament in Modern English,* Revised Edition. © J. B. Phillips 1958, 1960, 1972.

[2]A. W. Tozer, *The Root of the Righteous* (Camp Hill: Christian Publications, 1955, 1986), 106.

[3]Ibid, 8.

[4]Charles Stanley, *The Wonderful Spirit Filled Life* (Nashville: Thomas Nelson, 1992), 59.

[5]Jim Downing, *Meditation* (Colorado Springs: NavPress, 1976), 15.

[6]Phillips, *The New Testament in Modern English.*

[7]Stanley, *The Wonderful Spirit Filled Life,* 64.

[8]Andrew Murray, *With Christ In the School of Prayer,* 1978. Used by permission of Whitaker House, 30 Hunt Valley Circle, New Kensington, PA 15068.

The Tree of Life Illustration
Genesis 2:16-17; Genesis 3:6-7; Genesis 3:22-24

The premise for cults and other religions is simple: if a person commits an evil deed, he must do a good deed to make up for it. Sometimes we make Christianity look like this. We sin, we feel bad, and finally we purpose in our hearts to do something good to make up for our sin. It seems to be an endless cycle. We can illustrate this with a passage of Scripture which takes us back to the garden of Eden.

The tree from which Adam and Eve ate is not the tree of the knowledge of evil. It is the tree of the knowledge of good and evil. Do you see? *Good and evil come from the same tree.* When Adam and Eve ate from the tree, they were rejected. If we divide the tree in half and imagine good fruit on one side and bad fruit on the other (as illustrated) we can see how today we still eat from the same tree. We gossip or get drunk (eating the bad fruit), and then we go to church or read the Bible (eating the good fruit) to make up for it. But eating from either side produces the same result—rejection. (See verses on illustration.) So, what hope do we have of pleasing God? Answer: Eat from the *other* tree—The Tree of Life which represents Jesus. When we sin, instead of making up for it with a good deed, we must take that sin to Christ. He is just as sufficient for atoning for sin as He was in the day we accepted Him as Savior. Likewise, our good deeds are the overflow of His life in us rather than something we do in our flesh.

There is a "higher" *good* than the good which is produced within ourselves. And this brings us back to the first question of this week. Adam and Eve were *abiding in Christ.* This is the "higher" *good.* It is actually His good-

The Tree of the Knowledge of Good and Evil

Good Fruit   Bad Fruit

Isaiah 64:6   1 John 1:8

The Tree of Life

John 15:5

WEEK 5
IDOLATRY

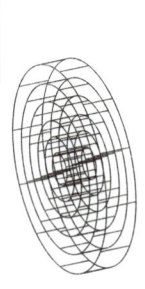

From this place also you shall go out With your hands on your head; For the Lord has rejected those in whom you trust, And you shall not prosper with them (Jer. 2:37).

DAY 1

What we usually think of when we think of an idol is a little statue that someone worships. We relate it to ourselves in terms of something that causes a mix-up of priorities. We identify the idols in our lives as those things which occupy the throne of our hearts. These all characterize the sin of idolatry. But there is a more subtle element that we often overlook.

Read Isaiah 44:6-20.

1. What does verse 6 say about God?

2. What do verses 9,11 say about the one who fashions an idol?

The word *precious* in verse 9 means "esteemed highly" or "of great value." It is one of the things that characterizes an idol—to give something the same value that God places upon us, those things which are most valuable to us.

3. What are some things in your life that are precious to you?

"False gods are not just idols in the fields or temples of an ancient, pagan time; they are living in our homes, deposited in our portfolio, fastened to the titles on our office doors, invested in the goals and plans of our self-generated lordship of our own destinies."[1]

4. Read verses 12 and 15. What does this man need?

5. The wood became an idol when . . .

❑ True ❑ False   It was planted as a tree. (v. 14)
❑ True ❑ False   It was burned to keep the man warm. (v. 15)
❑ True ❑ False   It was used to cook food. (vv. 15-16)
❑ True ❑ False   The man looked to it to deliver him. (v. 17)

Idolatry happens when we seek to have specific needs or problems met in something other than God.

Rebecca Manley Pippert defines an idol like this: "Anyone or anything we are committed to absolutely apart from God, or trusting in for our security other than God. Is there something we desperately want? Anything we feel we must have or life will lose its meaning? A person or object who represents for us a desire on which we would build our life instead of on God? That is what the Bible calls an idol."[3]

In today's passage, the man sought to have his needs (hunger, warmth) met from the wood. The wood could meet those needs. But it became an idol when the man sought something of it that only God could do—deliver him (v. 17).

How many times have you had a need for significance or self-esteem and sought to have it met in a person or in your ability? Or how many times have you neglected giving to God problems at home? Instead, perhaps you close the bedroom door, and turn the stereo up to drown them out. Maybe the music temporarily gave you a false sense of "escape," but did it deliver you? Did it solve the trouble in your heart brought on by your family crisis? And what about that person you look to to make you *feel* important or significant? Only God can provide long-lasting healthy self-esteem.

Idols may or may not be something tangible. Idols come in many forms.

6. **Look at your response to question 3. Which precious thing could become something to run to when you experience pressure?**

7. **What does idolatry do to a person's perspective of truth? (vv. 18-20)**

DAY 2

Today's passage compares the sufficiency of God with the futility of idols.

Read Psalm 135:5-18.

8. **What words establish the greatness of God in verses 5-7,13-14?**

9. **Verses 8-12 recounts God's work through the history of His people. How can the Holy Spirit use your memory of past experiences to keep you focused on Him and away from idols?**

10. **What words establish the worthlessness of idols in verses 15-17?**

11. **You've seen the warning signs on some product labels. Write a warning label that you could stick to the base of an idol. Use verse 18 as a guide.**

> "An idol is anything, other than Christ, which one runs to when under pressure. Whenever we are hurt, we must find some way of coping with that hurt. The thing that we run to when injured is our idol."[2]
> —Mike Wells

12. What does verse 18 indicate will happen to the person who trusts in the Lord?

DAY 3

Read Isaiah 46:1-11.

Bel has bowed down, Nebo stoops over (v. 1).

Bel was the patron god of Babylon. He was a sun-god. Nebo was also a Babylonian deity, the god of wisdom and learning. Isaiah exposes the inadequacies of these idols.

13. Why are these false gods and other idols inadequate remedies for distress or any other need? (vv. 1-2,7)

14. Why is another person limited in meeting our inner most needs? (indicated in vv. 3-4)

A wise man scales the city of the mighty, And brings down the stronghold in which they trust (Prov. 21:22).

An idol is also characterized in what or whom we place our trust.

15. What did God do to bring down the strongholds (idols) in which His people were placing their trust? (vv. 3-5,9)

16. Considering what you just wrote, what can you do to help others see that their idols are an insufficient source in meeting their needs?

17. Of the attributes God mentions in verses 3-5,9, which brings you the most confidence that He is able to meet any need? Why?

The following illustration uses today's passage to expose the inadequacy of idols in light of the perfection of God. As you look through these comparisons, think about how your own idols fit the descriptions in the right-hand column. Then cast these imperfections on the one and only perfect God.

God	Idols
Burden-Bearer (vv. 3-4)	Burdensome (vv. 1-2,7)
Carries us (v. 3)	We have to carry (v. 7)
Rescues us (v. 4)	Have to be rescued (v. 7)
Makes us (v. 4)	Have to be made (v. 6)
Is everywhere (v. 11)	Can't move (v. 7)
Saves us (v. 13)	Can't hear; can't save (v. 7)

DAY 4

Read Jeremiah 2:1-13.

"Those who regard vain idols Forsake their faithfulness" (Jonah 2:8).

In today's passage we see the Lord confronting His people through the prophet Jeremiah about their unfaithfulness to Him. They had forsaken Him to worship Baal, Asherah, the sun, the moon, and other idols.

18. **Where does idolatry lead a person? (vv. 5,8,11)**

19. **Verse 5—Think of a situation where you might think, *Hmm, it seems like God is being unfair or unjust here.* Write it below.**

20. **If you thought these things were actually true, why would it be easy to run to idols to meet your needs?**

21. **What had the Lord done to gain the father's trust according to the following verses?**

    Verse 6

    Verse 7

22. **How does our concept of God affect our tendency toward idolatry?**

23. **Verse 13—What are the "two evils" God refers to?**

24. **For each need or problem listed below list a broken cistern (v. 13) or idol that people run to instead of to God. An example is provided.**

Need/Problem	Broken Cistern
Love	Sex
Righteousness	
Rejection	
Acceptance	
Verbal abuse	
Self-esteem	
Stress	

25. **What does it mean that God is your "Fountain of Living Waters"?**

"There are stages in life when there is no storm, no crisis, when we do our human best; it is when a crisis arises that we instantly reveal upon whom we rely. If we have been learning to worship God and to trust Him, the crisis will reveal that we will go to the breaking point and not break in our confidence in Him."[5]
—Oswald Chambers

> "The secret unlocked in the Bible, that is revealed so vividly through the resurrection, is that the love we seek so desperately in the flesh can *ultimately* only be satisfied in the spirit. Indeed, the more ferociously we try to fill our need in our own way, the more frustrated we will become and the more likely it will become an obsession, creating an even deeper hunger than we had in the first place."[6]
> —Rebecca Manley Pippert

Read Genesis 3:1-13.

This is a familiar account and a portion of one of the passages we looked at last week. While it primarily depicts the fall of man, it also has a lesson for us in regard to idolatry.

26. Verse 6—What drew Eve to the tree?

27. What is the true source of goodness, delight, and wisdom?

28. Verse 7—What did Adam and Eve realize to be their problem?

29. How did they deal with their problem? (vv. 7-8)

30. What had sin done to their concept of God? (v. 10)

31. When Adam and Eve used fig leaves to cover their shame, the leaves became an idol. When they ran to the trees to hide their sin, the trees became an idol. Explain how an unhealthy concept of God might have impacted their actions.

32. Eve was correct when she said that the serpent had deceived her (v. 13). He deceived her in regard to what God was like and in regard to His Word (vv. 4-5). Which lies of Satan in regard to God's character might cause you to run to an idol? (refer to question 19)

33. Identify the idols in your life which God has exposed through the course of this study. Write them in the space below.

[1] *Lord of the Impossible*, Lloyd John Ogilvie, 1984 Abingdon Press. Used by permission.
[2] Mike Wells, *Sidetracked In the Wilderness* (New York: Fleming H. Revell a division of Baker Book House Company, 1991), 43.
[3] Rebecca Manley Pippert, *Hope Has Its Reasons* (Westmont: InterVarsity Press, 1989), 170.
[4] Oswald Chambers, *My Utmost For His Highest* (Westwood: Barbour and Company Inc., 1935, 1963), 164.
[5] Ibid, 164-165.
[6] Rebecca Manley Pippert, *Hope Has Its Reasons*, 126.

WEEK 6
GOD IS NOT A MAN

DAY 1

Last week we studied that even as Christians we have the tendency to run to various idols when the pressure is on or when we are in need. One of the reasons we do this is because we do not have a true concept of God.

David L. Hocking writes, "It is very often the limited understanding of God or the myths people believe about God that makes them turn away from Him or be fearful to trust Him."[1]

We may perceive God as too small to handle our problems or too big to care about them. These ideas are not based on truth. Consciously or unconsciously we tend to give attributes of ourselves and other humans to God.

"God is not a man, that He should lie, Nor a son of man, that He should repent; Has He said, and will He not do it? Or has He spoken, and will He not make good?" (Num. 23:19).

"Also the Glory of Israel will not lie or change His mind; for He is not a man that He should change His mind" (1 Sam. 15:29).

1. **The left column lists the deeds of men. Beside each corresponding verse write what Scripture reveals about God, as compared to man.**

Man	God
Willfully hurts	Lamentations 3:22-23; Psalm 103:8
Remembers failures	Isaiah 43:25; Psalm 103:12
Forgets efforts	Hebrews 6:10
Changes	Hebrews 13:8; James 1:17
Is full of sin	1 John 3:5; Hebrews 7:26
Untrustworthy/unfaithful	Psalm 111:7-8; Psalm 89:34
Loves conditionally	Romans 5:8; 1 John 4:10
Fallible/undependable	Deuteronomy 31:8
Limited knowledge	Psalm 139:1-2; Hebrews 4:13
Dies	John 5:24; John 11:25-26

2. **Look again at the left column. Place an "X" beside the one characteristic of man that you are most likely to attribute to God.**

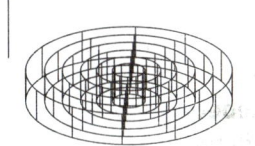

In the remainder of the study we will look at four different concepts of God in which we fashion after man-like images.

DAY 2

In his book, *Your God Is Too Small*,[3] J. B. Phillips characterizes several concepts of God which are not based upon the biblical revelation of who He is but upon our own limited imaginations. The remainder of this week contains four reworked composites of those concepts.

"My Old Man"

Your experiences in early childhood often shape your view of everything. Your values, desires, interests, personal habits (from the way you tie your shoe to the number of times you brush your teeth in a day) are all to a large degree dependent upon the patterns set for you as a child. Never is this more true than in the area of your view of authority. And this usually comes back to your father. If your father was a domineering individual, your view of an authority figure is usually one of cold harshness or criticism. If he was warm and loving, you are usually more receptive to the voice of authority, and so forth. Sociologists see it played out in the work place and in schools. Psychologists deal with many clients who blame their problems on childhood experiences.

God often takes it on the chin because of our preconceived notions of how He loves, responds and commands. He is viewed through the lens of past human experience and predetermined to react like our authorities react. But God is not a man. He wants us to understand what this means in our relationship to Him. The mature one will be the one who outgrows the concept of God as "My Old Man."

J. B. Phillips writes, "The early conception of God is almost invariably founded upon the child's idea of his father. If he is lucky enough to have a good father this is all to the good, provided of course that the conception of God grows with the rest of personality. But if the child is afraid (or, worse still, afraid and feeling guilty because he is afraid) of his own father, the chances are that his Father in Heaven will appear to him a fearful Being. Again, if he is lucky, he will outgrow this conception, and indeed differentiate between his early 'fearful' idea and his later mature conception. But many are not able to outgrow the sense of guilt and fear, and in adult years are still obsessed with it, although it has actually nothing to do with their real relationship with the living God."[4]

3. **What would happen if we embraced the "My Old Man" concept of God—that God is likened to our earthly father? Complete the column on the right based on the descriptions on the left.**

If an earthly father is:	A person might perceive God as
Critical	demanding or hard to please
Unaffectionate	
Gone (divorce or death)	
Temperamental	
Lax in disciplining	

4. **What images of God come to mind when you pray, "Our Father, who art in heaven ..." as Jesus commanded in Matthew 6:9?**

5. **What does God want to reveal about Himself with the title "Father"?**

6. **Look up the following passages and write what they reveal about both your earthly father and your Heavenly Father.**

Earthly father	Heavenly Father
Psalm 27:10	
Isaiah 49:15	
Hebrews 12:9-10	

Just as a father has compassion on his children, So the Lord has compassion on those who fear Him (Ps. 103:13).

Things we observe in our parents do not always have a negative effect in our concept of God. Many are blessed with loving parents, which has a positive impact in the way they see the Heavenly Father. But no earthly father is perfect. We must thank God for the parents He has given us and forgive them of their imperfections. Take time to identify qualities of your father which you attribute to God and discern if they are true of Him or not. Thank God that He is Father to you and your parents. Leave behind the "My Old Man" concept as you deepen your relationship with Him.

DAY 3

"The Elder Statesman"

It is easy to find a member of Congress re-elected more on the basis that he has always been there than on his merit as a progressive mover and shaker. Many people view God this way. From their earliest memories they have pictured God as an old man, an elder statesman sitting on his throne, issuing decrees of judgments upon the people on earth. He is respected, even feared, but not seen as one that is necessarily in touch with modern events. He speaks only the king's English and uses terms like "sin" and "repent" that seem archaic by today's standards. He is respected, but seldom upheld as the one true God, to be worshiped and praised.

7. **Under the correct heading record attributes each verse assigns to God and/or man.**

	Man	God
Psalm 102:24-27		
Isaiah 40:28-30		
Isaiah 46:4		
Isaiah 51:6		

8. **Record your thoughts about these attributes.**

"Jesus taught us to address God familiarly as 'Our Father,' but he added to that the qualifying phrase, 'who art in heaven,' so that we might always be aware of the remoteness, the otherness and the transcendence of the God who allows us to experience him here on earth."[5]
—Leonard Griffith

9. List a temptation you face that you feel God is unable to understand.

We do not have a high priest who cannot sympathize with our weaknesses, but one who has been tempted in all things as we are, yet without sin (Heb. 4:15).

10. How does the above verse speak to you in light of what you wrote?

It is sometimes hard to believe that a God who was involved in the lives of chariot racers thousands of years ago can keep up with the pace of today's computer generation, especially if a person has Him locked into the image of "The Elder Statesman." Think through your own concept of God and see if any of the wrong ideas discussed in today's study still linger in your mind. Lay to rest "The Elder Statesman."

DAY 4

"The CEO"

The Chief Executive Officer of a corporation is a busy man. He hardly has time to learn the names of his employees and he certainly isn't concerned with the details, only the big picture. He has a vast empire which needs constant attention and he can't be bothered with the needs of individuals in his organization. Sound like the God of some people you know? God can't possibly be interested in them, because there are bigger problems for him to solve. He is simply too busy and after all, He can only be in one place at one time. Right? With a phone receiver in each ear and three other people on hold, when does he have time to hear the requests of the little guy? He is like the captain, who knows his sergeants well, but has little, if any knowledge of the privates' names. If they want God's attention, it depends upon them. And in this misconception, people live their entire lives never experiencing God's constant and consuming love.

Read Psalm 139:1-18.

11. When was/is the Lord thinking about you according to these verses?

Verse 2

Verse 3

Verse 4

Verse 13

Verse 15

Verse 16

God is ... A very present help in trouble (Ps. 46:1).

12. Read Psalm 139:7-12. What does it mean that God is a "present help"?

Thou hast enclosed me behind and before, and laid Thy hand upon me (v. 5).

13. Read Psalm 139:5. Where do you picture yourself? (check one)

- ❏ Imprisoned with a parole officer checking every time you mess up.
- ❏ Squashed underneath a hand of expectations you can't live up to.
- ❏ In a shelter where nothing can harm you and where you have the Lord all to yourself.

"Am I a God who is near," declares the Lord, "And not a God far off? Can a man hide himself in hiding places, So I do not see him?" declares the Lord. "Do I not fill the heavens and the earth?" declares the Lord (Jer. 23:23-24).

14. What can you "know" and "not know" according to today's passage?

DAY 5

"A Guy Like Me"

Have you ever heard someone say, "I don't think Jesus would have a problem with going to a bar" or something similar? "I don't think Jesus would be so hard on everybody as some Christians I know." "Jesus had long hair, so why can't I?" The problem with these questions and/or statements is not in their truth or deception but in their concept of Christ. Most people don't have a problem with Jesus. And the reason they don't, is that in the end, Jesus looks a lot like them. If a person doesn't like alcohol, then, for example, his Jesus is hard on alcoholics. On the other hand, if the person isn't very offended by pornography, then neither is his Jesus. Jesus becomes opposed to the sins we are against and turns his head in apathy to the sins we find tolerable and are so often guilty of committing. But Jesus is neither most like my concept of him or your concept of him. Jesus is most like the Bible's concept of Him. Jesus isn't just a better guy than most; He is God. There is no better way to rationalize my sin than to make Jesus look like a slightly larger and nicer image of myself. For this reason, God seems inadequate in times of distress and need. What I can't handle, God can't handle. Therein lies the danger of looking at God as if he is a "A Guy Like Me."

Read Matthew 5:21-22,27-28 and James 2:10-11.

15. How is sin described in these passages?

16. **What do the passages indicate about the categories of sin?**

17. **Which sin(s) is/are the hardest for you to tolerate in other people?**

18. **Which sin(s) is/are the easiest for you to tolerate in yourself?**

19. **Of the sins that you listed, which does God hate the most?**

20. **When have you ever embraced the "Guy Like Me" concept of God?**

21. **Read Psalm 130:3-4. Who has the only right to look down on someone because of sin in his/her life?**

22. **Yet, how does He respond to the sinner? (v. 4)**

23. **How does this verse affect the psalmist's concept of God? (v. 4)**

24. **How does it affect your own concept?**

25. **Which of the following best describes the god in your imagination?**

    ❏ My Old Man
    ❏ The Elder Statesman
    ❏ The CEO
    ❏ A Guy Like Me

26. **Why did you make your choice?**

Obviously, false concepts of God are not limited to these four images. We will examine many other concepts throughout the remainder of the year as we discover who the One True God is and what He is really like.

27. **Go back through the study and find a verse or phrase that has real meaning for you in revealing what God is like. Write it in the margin.**

[1]*The Nature of God in Plain Language*, David L. Hocking, 1984, Word Publishing, Nashville, Tennessee. All rights reserved.
[2]Walter T. Conner, *The Gospel of Redemption* (Nashville: Broadman Press, 1945), 52.
[3]J. B. Phillips, *Your God Is Too Small* (New York: Macmillan Publishing, 1956), 19-20.
[4]Ibid., 14-15.
[5]*God In Man's Experience*, Leonard Griffith, 1968, Word Publishing, Nashville, Tennessee. All rights reserved.

Below are the answers to the first question for this week. They form an acrostic that spells "Christlike." This is an illustration that you will refer to throughout the rest of this study to equip you in how to share what the character of God is like. Be wholehearted in your memory work, especially on weeks that include verses for this illustration. This week's verses are the first on the illustration, "God Is Not a Man."

God Is Not a Man
(Num. 23:19; 1 Sam. 15:29; 1 Cor. 1:25)

Man		God
Willfully hurts	Lamentations 3:22-23; Psalm 103:8; Matthew 9:36 . . .	Compassionate
Remembers failures	Isaiah 43:25; Psalm 103:12; Micah 7:19	Harbors no grudge
Forgets efforts	Hebrews 6:10	Remembers your efforts
Changes	Hebrews 13:8; James 1:17; Isaiah 54:10	Immutable
Is full of sin	1 John 3:5; Hebrews 7:26; Hebrews 4:15	Sinless
Untrustworthy/unfaithful	Psalm 111:7-8; Psalm 89:34; 1 Kings 8:23	Trustworthy/faithful
Loves conditionally	Romans 5:8; 1 John 4:10; Romans 8:38-39	Loves unconditionally
Fallible/undependable	Deuteronomy 31:8	Infallible/dependable
Limited knowledge	Psalm 139:1-2; Hebrews 4:13; Proverbs 15:3	Knows all
Dies	John 5:24; John 11:25-26; John 6:40	Eternal

God became man in the Person of Jesus Christ as a revelation of His nature.

Jesus Christ
John 1:14; Colossians 1:15; Hebrews 1:3

God Is Not a Man Illustration, David Stephens *Discovering Who He Is,* (Tulsa: D-Vine Focus, 1989), 1.

THE BIBLE, GOD'S WORD

SCRIPTURE MEMORY
The Bible
■ 2 Timothy 3:16
■ Hebrews 4:12
■ 2 Peter 1:20-21

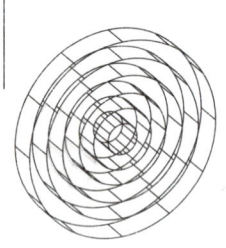

Thy words were found and I ate them, And Thy words became for me a joy and the delight of my heart; For I have been called by Thy name, O Lord God of hosts (Jer. 15:16).

Charles Stanley writes, "The Bible is the mind of God in print. It gives men and women a purpose for living. It explains the mysteries of creation, suffering, heaven and hell. The Bible holds the keys for attaining and maintaining real success. It contains the blueprint for successful marriage and family relationships. The Scriptures contain the story of salvation, a story that reaches back to the beginning of time and extends into eternity."[1]

We can understand how the Bible comes to us as a divine book by looking at *Revelation, Inspiration*, and *Illumination*.

Revelation
God unveils or discloses Himself through nature, history and even within man himself. This is called *General Revelation.* Yet there are truths that are not made known by General Revelation such as God's redeeming work in Christ. So God gave to us the *Special Revelation* in the Scriptures. The Bible reiterates the truths proclaimed in nature, history, and so forth, but it also declares the salvation that God has provided for mankind in Jesus Christ.

Inspiration
As God revealed Himself to the sacred writers through His Holy Spirit, they wrote down what He spoke to them. Based upon the supernatural influence of God in their lives, their writings are given divine trustworthiness. When we look at *Inspiration*, as used here, we understand it to mean that the writers presented what was spoken to them in their own language and personality.

Illumination
Illumination continues today as the Holy Spirit gives us insight and understanding into what is in the Bible. A person cannot understand the god-given revelation of His Word without the *Illumination* of the Holy Spirit. You cannot read a book in the dark, but when you turn on the light, you can read it. *Illumination* turns on the light in understanding the Scripture.

DAY 1

The Bible was written over a period of approximately 1,400 years, originally in three languages: the Old Testament primarily in Hebrew with a small section in Aramaic, and the New Testament in Greek. It was penned by 40 authors from many walks of life—kings, common people, philosophers, fishermen, scholars, the uneducated, poets, farmers, statesmen, carpenters. Writers, most of whom knew nothing of each other, all wrote about one theme—the redemption of man through God's chosen One—Jesus Christ.

1. What do we learn about the Bible from the following verses?

Psalm 119:89

Psalm 119:151-152

Psalm 119:160

2 Timothy 3:16-17

Hebrews 4:12

2 Peter 1:20-21

2. What does Jesus say about the Scriptures?

Mark 13:31

John 6:63

John 8:31-32

John 17:17

"It is not an idle word for you; indeed it is your life" (Deut. 32:47).

3. If a car is idling, it's running but not going anywhere. Why is the Bible "not an idle word"?

4. What does the Bible "is your life" mean?

5. Look again at 2 Timothy 3:16-17 and Hebrews 4:12. What is said in these verses to indicate that the Bible is "not an idle word"?

DAY 2

Today's lesson examines why its prophecies and fulfillments make the Bible unique to all other books.

6. On the next page are Old Testament prophecies about Jesus. Match the New Testament Scripture fulfillment to each prophetic passage.

____ They divided my garments among them, And for my clothing they cast lots (Ps. 22:18).

____ He keeps all his bones; Not one of them is broken (Ps. 34:20).

____ They also gave me gall for my food, And for my thirst they gave me vinegar to drink (Ps. 69:21).

____ "Therefore the Lord Himself will give you a sign: Behold, a virgin will be with child and bear a son, and she will call His name Immanuel" (Isa. 7:14).

____ Then a shoot will spring from the stem of Jesse, And a branch from his roots will bear fruit (Isa. 11:1). (Jesse is the earthly father of David.)

____ A voice is calling, "Clear the way for the Lord in the wilderness; Make smooth in the desert a highway for our God" (Isa. 40:3).

____ Surely our griefs He Himself bore, And our sorrows He carried; Yet we ourselves esteemed Him stricken, Smitten of God, and afflicted. But He was pierced through for our transgressions, He was crushed for our iniquities; The chastening for our well-being fell upon Him, And by His scourging we are healed (Isa. 53:4-6).

____ "As for you, Bethlehem Ephrathah, Too little to be among the clans of Judah, From you One will go forth for Me to be ruler in Israel. His goings forth are from long ago" (Mic. 5:2).

____ Rejoice greatly, O daughter of Zion! Shout in triumph, O daughter of Jerusalem! Behold, your king is coming to you; He is just and endowed with salvation, Humble, and mounted on a donkey, Even on a colt, the foal of a donkey (Zech. 9:9).

A. Luke 2:4,6-7
B. Matthew 21:2,4-5
C. Luke 1:31-33
D. Matthew 3:1-3
E. Matthew 27:35
F. Matthew 1:18-25
G. Matthew 27:34,48
H. John 19:33,36
I. 2 Corinthians 5:21

7. How does this activity help you understand the reliability of the Scripture?

8. Fulfillment of prophecy is one way the Bible is set apart from other books. How else have you seen the difference between the Bible and other books?

9. How did the psalmist find the Bible to be reliable in his life?

Psalm 119:50

Psalm 119:66-67

Psalm 119:92

Psalm 119:93

Psalm 119:144

Psalm 119:165

DAY 3

The attitude of the disciple toward his Bible is important. It is not a book with pages of mere *suggestions* from which we pick and choose the ones to make applicable to our lives. It is a book of *commandments* on which we base all decisions. It is "living and active." The Bible was given to be applied, to be lived out, to *do*.

"If you know these things, you are blessed if you do them" (John 13:17).

"Not the hearers of the Law are just before God, but the doers of the Law will be justified" (Rom. 2:13).

Prove yourselves doers of the word, and not merely hearers who delude themselves (Jas. 1:22).

10. Write your week 1 memory verse ("Lordship of Christ").

11. Read Luke 6:46. Who does Jesus imply is the person who has truly made Him Lord?

Read Matthew 7:24-27.

12. Check the differences the person in verses 24-25 experienced as compared to the person in verses 26-27.

❏ The amount of the Word they heard.
❏ The foundation their houses were built upon.
❏ The storms that blew against their houses.
❏ The end result.

13. Why did one house stand and the other fall?

14. According to this passage why do some Christians live victoriously even in the middle of the storms of life, while others crumble in the middle of adversity?

15. Write down the words or phrases the psalmist uses to indicate that the Bible is to be applied.

Psalm 119:35

Psalm 119:44

Psalm 119:59-60

Psalm 119:101

Psalm 119:133

Psalm 119:166

16. Sometimes we approach the Bible in hopes of gaining new insight into some spiritual truth when what we need to do is concentrate on things we already know we should be doing but are not. Write something that God has taught you but which you have not applied.

17. What does today's study encourage you to do in light of this?

Today we will look at the five methods of grasping God's Word: Hearing, Reading, Studying, Memorizing, and Meditating.

So faith comes from hearing, and hearing by the word of Christ (Rom. 10:17).

18. What elements and/or benefits of hearing the Word do you see in the following verses?

Psalm 119:2

Psalm 119:130

Blessed is he who reads and those who hear the words of the prophecy, and heed the things which are written in it (Rev. 1:3).

19. What elements and/or benefits of reading the Word do you see in the following verses?

Psalm 119:7

Psalm 119:104

Now these were more noble-minded than those in Thessalonica, for they received the word with great eagerness, examining the Scriptures daily, to see whether these things were so (Acts 17:11).

20. What elements and/or benefits of studying the Bible do you see in the following verses?

Psalm 119:18

Psalm 119:33

Psalm 119:45

Psalm 119:125

"Please receive instruction from His mouth, And establish His words in your heart" (Job 22:22).

21. What elements and/or benefits of memorizing the Bible do you see in the following verses?

Psalm 119:11

Psalm 119:16

Psalm 119:42

Psalm 119:52

Psalm 119:61

Psalm 119:93

Psalm 119:141

Psalm 119:176

"This book of the law shall not depart from your mouth, but you shall meditate on it day and night, so that you may be careful to do according to all that is written in it; for then you will make your way prosperous, and then you will have success" (Josh. 1:8).

22. What elements and/or benefits of meditating upon the Bible do you see in the following verses?

Psalm 119:15

Psalm 119:23

Psalm 119:27

Psalm 119:38

Psalm 119:48

Psalm 119:55

Psalm 119:97

Psalm 119:99

Psalm 119:148

23. Which of the five methods of grasping God's Word do you struggle with the most?

24. Find a verse in Psalm 119 which helps you give this struggle to God. Write the verse below.

DAY 5

Prior to planting his crops, the farmer does all that he can to prepare the soil so that the seeds take root, grow, and produce vegetables or fruit. God is the One who causes the seeds to grow and yet He will not do what he expects the farmer to do: fertilize, weed, and so forth. Could it be that the soil of our hearts needs some preparation too, so that the Word will take root in our lives? Today's parable breaks up the ground of our heart.

Read Mark 4:1-20.

25. What is the purpose of planting a seed?

26. What is the purpose of planting the Word in our lives?

27. What happens to the seed sown beside the road? (v. 15)

28. What happens to the seed sown on the rocky places? (vv. 16-17)

29. What happens to the seed sown among the thorns? (vv. 18-19)

30. What happens to the seed sown in the good soil? (v. 20)

31. In this parable the soil determined the seed's fruitfulness. If God's Word is the seed, why is it that not everyone responds the same way to His Word?

32. Check the following hindrances which get in your way the most and keep the Word from becoming fruitful.

   ❑ Lack of rooting
   ❑ Affliction and persecution
   ❑ Worries of the world
   ❑ Deceitfulness of riches
   ❑ Desire for other things

33. Read verses 15-20 again. Which soil describes you? Write today's date in your Bible beside the verse that describes you.

34. What is the greatest hindrance to your becoming like one of those described in verse 20?

---

[1]Charles Stanley, *The Wonderful Spirit Filled Life* (Nashville: Thomas Nelson, 1992), 207.

METHODS OF BIBLE STUDY (1 & 2 PETER)

SCRIPTURE MEMORY
Applying the Word
■ James 1:22

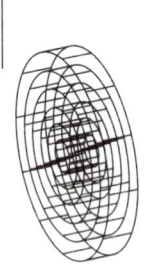

DAY 1

After studying the importance of grasping God's Word, the Bible, last week, we now turn our attention to different methods of personal Bible study, and the importance of application.

Ezra had set his heart to study the law of the Lord, and to practice it, and to teach His statutes and ordinances in Israel (Ezra 7:10).

Ezra made it his ambition to:
1. Study the Bible.
2. Put into practice what he had learned.
3. Pass on what he had learned to others.

Ezra set a good example for us as disciples of Jesus. A disciple increases his knowledge of the Scripture so that he can apply it to his own life and then he passes it on to someone else. We do not study the Bible with the sole purpose of teaching others. Ezra taught only after he had studied and applied.

A disciple always looks for ways he can make what he has learned and applied "pass-on-able": "The things which you have heard from me in the presence of many witnesses, these entrust to faithful men, who will be able to teach others also" (2 Tim. 2:2). The methods you will learn this week can easily be passed along to another growing Christian.

Read Proverbs 1:1-7.

1. Verse 2—What is the difference between wisdom and knowledge?

2. List five reasons why Bible study is important.

1.

2.

3.

4.

5.

3. Verse 7—What is needed before you can acquire spiritual knowledge?

4. Write your week 7 memory verse ("The Bible").

As you begin to do personal Bible study pray for yourself as Paul prayed for the Ephesians in Ephesians 1:18, "I pray that the eyes of your heart may be enlightened, so that you may know what is the hope of His calling, what are the riches of the glory of His inheritance in the saints."

5. Write your week 3 memory verse ("The Holy Spirit").

Remember, that the Holy Spirit is your teacher. He is the One who will show you specific areas in your life that He wants to change.

DAY 2

Ready, Aim, Fire Method

Ready—*Bring the principles into focus.* Write points or facts the passage reveals.
Aim—*Finding the target.* What verse stands out to you most?
Fire—*What does my "target verse" challenge me to do?* How can I put into practice what this verse is saying? What specific commitment do I need to make to live out the truth of this verse?

1 Peter 1 (An Example)
Ready—*Bring the principles into focus.*

Peter greets other Christians with his letter. (vv. 1-3)

Because of Christ's resurrection, they have received an inheritance which is everlasting and cannot fade away. (vv. 3-5)

Their souls are secure, they are able to endure temporary trials and persecutions with joy, knowing the goal is praise and honor of Christ.(vv. 6-9)

Christ's suffering was prophesied by Old Testament prophets. (vv. 10-12)

Put aside what they were and become holy, keeping their hope set on Christ. (vv. 13-16)

Don't take their salvation lightly, it was a costly gift, paid by the blood of Jesus, who was known before the beginning of time, came to the world, died, was resurrected that they might have faith in God. (vv. 17-21)

Peter compares this gift to an imperishable seed. (vv. 22-25)

Aim—*Finding the target.*

Verse 22

Fire—*What does my "target verse" challenge me to do?*

Since I have been given this "imperishable seed" (v. 23) I have the capacity through Christ to let that love "bloom" with everyone. This verse convicts me not to take for granted other Christians. I will pray now, thanking God for my friend Olivia who always encourages me in my walk with Christ. I will also write her a note thanking her for her friendship, expressing my love.

1 Peter 2 (Your Turn)

Ready—*Bring the principles into focus.*

Aim—*Finding the target.*

Fire—*What does my "target verse" challenge me to do?*

DAY 3

The P's and Q's Method

P's-*Principles.* Write down the principles the passage teaches.
Q's-*Questions.* Answer the following questions in regard to the principles you discovered in the passage.

    What sin do I need to confess?
    What example do I need to model?
    What command do I need to obey?

Application. Upon answering the questions, what action do I need to take?

1 Peter 3 (An Example)

P's-*Principles*

Peter continues his admonition of a servant's heart from chapter 2. He emphasizes the reward of the submissive wife: that her husband will respond in his commitment to God. (vv. 1-2)

The value of hidden beauty, gentleness, a quiet spirit, is precious to God and is eternal as opposed to external beauty, hair, clothes, jewelry. (vv. 3-4)

He reminds his readers that the examples of godly women of times past were submissive, specifically, Sarah who submitted to Abraham. (vv. 5-6)

Verse 7—Peter admonishes husbands to recognize the differences between them and their wives, physically and the equality of women, spiritually, being fellow heirs of grace.

Peter gives an overall picture of what a submissive spirit will look like: harmonious, sympathetic, brotherly, kindhearted, humble, a controlled tongue, righteous deeds. (vv. 8-12)

If submission brings suffering then it is to be considered a blessing, responding on the basis of Christ's lordship of our lives, not the intimidation and fear of the opponent. (vv. 13-15)

Verse 16—Clear conscience will put to shame those who revile good behavior.

Verse 17—Suffering can result from doing what is right or wrong. But it's better to suffer for what is right.

Verse 18—Christ suffered to the point of death. The perfect for the imperfect so that He could bring us to God.

Verse 21—Spiritual baptism brings salvation through the resurrection of Jesus Christ.

Verse 22—Jesus is at the right hand of God, everything is subjected to Him.

Q's–Questions

What sin do I need to confess? Verse 9—I need to refrain from returning evil for evil and insult for insult. Sometimes I play the cut down game with other Christians. Even though it is teasing it does not build up or edify.

What example do I need to model? I need to follow the example of Sarah who concentrated more on a quiet and submissive heart (her inner beauty) rather than her external appearance. Vanity is a waste of time. (vv. 4-6)

What command do I need to obey? Verse 15—I need to obey this command in the area of witnessing. Today I had an opportunity to identify with Christ, verbally, and I kept my mouth shut. I sense God is leading me back to the person I was talking with to set up another time together. Maybe God will graciously give me another chance with him.

Application

I tend to think of a submissive spirit as "obeying with no questions asked." No wonder "submissive" has such a negative connotation for me. But, when I look at how Peter characterizes it, I realize it encompasses all of Christian behavior, inwardly and outwardly. For me, a lack of a submissive spirit seems to be manifesting itself mostly in my speech. I was too abrasive to Elaine today. They were not responses based upon Christ's lordship of my life but to "get her back" for unintentionally hurting my feelings with her remarks about my clothes. I will apologize to her for my attitude without trying to manipulate an apology from her.

1 Peter 4 (Your Turn)

P's–*Principles*

Q's–*Questions*

What sin do I need to confess?

What example do I need to model?

What command do I need to obey?

Application

DAY 4

The Triple S Method

Standard—State the principle or ideal expressed from one particular verse.
Struggles—How am I not measuring up to this (ideal or principle) in my life?
Strategy—My course of action to change this. How can I apply the Scripture to my problem?

1 Peter 5 (An Example)

Standard—Verse 6. It says for me to humble myself and let God exalt me.

Struggles—I am too boastful about my athletic ability. I tend to take over as "coach" even when we're playing around just for fun. And I get frustrated too easily with others who don't have the natural ability I have.

Strategy—I need to apologize to Bill whom I embarrassed on the court the other day, and I just need to have a more Christlike attitude of putting other's interests ahead of myself.

2 Peter 1 (Your Turn)

Standard

Struggles

Strategy

DAY 5

The John 15:5 Method

1. "I am the Vine"—What does this passage reveal about God or Jesus Christ?
2. "You are the branches"—What does this passage reveal about me?
3. "He who abides in Me and I in Him bears much fruit"—What verse from this passage is the Holy Spirit using to prune me so that His fruit can be produced in my life?
4. "For apart from Me you can do nothing"—Pray the following:

Lord, I realize that the first step in applying this truth in my life is to admit that without You I cannot do it. So, I give this to You right now and thank You that no matter what happens, You have taken it. Let me not listen to the voice of the deceiver, who wants me to feel defeated. Let me not trust in my own strength and try to accomplish this in my flesh. But may I place my hope and my trust in You that through Jesus You can accomplish this in me. Amen.

2 Peter 2 (An Example)

1. "I am the vine"—What does this passage reveal about God or Jesus Christ?

Verse 4—He did not spare angels when they sinned by casting them into hell.

Verse 5—He did not spare the ancient world and brought a flood upon the ungodly.

Verse 6—He condemned the cities of Sodom and Gomorrah to destruction as an example to those who would live ungodly afterwards.

Verse 7—He rescued righteous Lot.

Verse 9—He knows how to rescue the godly from temptation and to keep the unrighteous under judgments.

2. "You are the branches"—what does this passage reveal about me?

Verses 1-3—I am not immune as a Christian to being exploited by false teachers.

Verses 10-22—I am not immune to sin or to making sin my lifestyle. I have the capability of going back to the lifestyle I knew before Christ.

3. "He who abides in Me and I in Him bears much fruit"—What verse from this passage is the Holy Spirit using to prune me so that His fruit can be produced in my life?

This passage reminds me again of how much God hates sin. It also reminds me again of how vulnerable I am toward sin. Verse 19 says, "promising them freedom while they themselves are slaves of corruption; for by what a man is overcome, by this he is enslaved." One sin I really enjoy is gossiping. (It's a big step calling it by its right name!) When two of my friends and I get together we talk about our frustrations with other people. I realize that instead of being "fun" this sin is really enslaving me, because I can't seem to quit. I will call my friends now and tell them what I've learned and maybe the three of us can stop gossiping altogether (John 15:5).

4. "Apart from Me, you can do nothing"—Pray the following:

Lord, I realize that the first step in applying this truth in my life is to admit that without You I cannot do it. So, I give this to You right now and thank You that no matter what happens, You have taken it. Let me not listen to the voice of the deceiver, who wants me to feel defeated. Let me not trust in my own strength and try to accomplish this in my flesh. But may I place my hope and my trust in You that through Jesus You can accomplish all things in me. Amen.

2 Peter 3 (Your Turn)

1. "I am the Vine"—What is this saying about God or Jesus Christ?

2. "You are the branches"—What does this passage reveal about me?

3. "He who abides in Me and I in Him bears much fruit"—What verse from this passage is the Holy Spirit using to prune me so that His fruit can be produced in my life?

4. "For apart from Me you can do nothing"—Pray the following.

Lord, I realize that the first step in applying this truth in my life is to admit that without You I cannot do it. So, I give this to You right now and thank You that no matter what happens, You have taken it. Let me not listen to the voice of the deceiver, who wants me to feel defeated. Let me not trust my own strength and try to accomplish this in my flesh. But may I place my hope and my trust in You that through Jesus You can accomplish all things in me. Amen.

THE COMPASSION OF GOD

"The Good Shepherd protects his sheep against the wolf, and instead of fleeing he gives his life for the sheep. He knows them all by name and loves them. He knows their distress and their weakness. He heals the wounded, gives drink to the thirsty, sets upright the falling, and leads them gently, not sternly, to pasture. He leads them on the right way. He seeks the one lost sheep, and brings it back to the fold."[1]

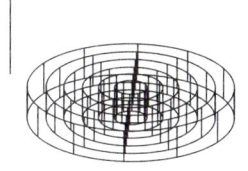

DAY 1

1. Why did Jesus feel compassion according to the following verses?

Matthew 9:36

Matthew 14:14-21

Matthew 15:32

Read Luke 15:11-32.

The parable of the prodigal son is probably the most well known and referred to of the parables Jesus taught. Interestingly enough it is really the Father who is the central figure here rather than the lost son. This parable has much to teach us about God and about ourselves.

2. What did the younger son do with his inheritance? (vv. 13-14)

3. What caused the son to want to return home? (vv. 14,16)

4. What impresses you about the way the father responds in verse 20?

5. "I am no longer worthy to be called your son (v. 21)." What does this phrase reveal was the younger son's attitude before he left home?

6. If you were the father, how would you respond to the younger son's response in verse 21?

7. How does the father respond? (vv. 22-24)

8. What was the attitude of the older son? (vv. 28-30)

9. What impresses you about the way the father responds? (vv. 31-32)

10. If you were the father, how would you respond to the older son?

11. How has your life paralleled the life of the younger son?

12. How has your life paralleled the life of the older son?

13. In week 6 we looked at what it means to see God as our Heavenly Father and not like our earthly father. How does today's study help you understand your Heavenly Father?

DAY 2

The fog of affliction sometimes clouds our ability to sense God's presence. Yet, if what the Bible says is true, that God's lovingkindnesses never cease and that His compassions never fail, maybe our feelings are deceiving us. Perhaps the issue is not so much finding God in the mist, but understanding that it is in the mist that God is actually seeking us.

Read Lamentations 3:19-32.

14. When is God's compassion available to you? (vv. 22-23)

15. Why can you place your hope in a compassionate God? (vv. 21,24)

16. How do these verses speak to victims of affliction or injustice who may feel like God has forgotten them?

Verse 24

Verse 25

Verse 26

Verse 31

Verse 32

17. Do you think it is contradictory for a compassionate God to cause grief? Explain. (v. 32)

"Now God, who has made us, knows what we are and that our happiness lies in Him. Yet we will not seek it in Him as long as He leaves us any other resort where it can even plausibly be looked for. While what we call 'our own life' remains agreeable we will not surrender it to Him. What then can God do in our interests but make 'our own life' less agreeable to us, and take away the plausible sources of false happiness? It is just here, where God's providence seems at first to be most cruel, that the Divine humility, the stooping down of the Highest, most deserves praise. ... He will have us even though we have shown that we prefer everything else to Him, and come to Him because there is 'nothing better' now to be had... It is hardly complimentary to God that we should choose Him as an alternative to Hell: yet even this He accepts."[4]

18. Verse 32—On what basis does God extend His compassion?

DAY 3

As humans, we extend compassion to whom we deem is worthy of it. God's compassion extends beyond these limits because in the final analysis, none of us is worthy of it. Today's study helps us understand that God's compassion is based upon who God is, not who we are.

Read Psalm 103:1-14.

Forget none of His benefits (v. 2).

19. What are the benefits of being a child of God?

Verse 3

Verse 4

Verse 5

Verse 6

Verse 12

20. On what basis has He blessed you with these things? (vv. 8,11,13)

21. What is not the basis of these blessings? (v. 10)

"I am a father. I have four children...As a father, I want my children to learn as quickly as they can. If they come home with a bad report card, I am disappointed, but not as disappointed as I would be if they did not love each other. If I were a teacher focusing on grades only, then my concern would be grades. Because I am a father I would rather see C's for grades and have them love each other dearly than see A's with little or no love between them. If I were only a master of my household, then I would desire only their obedience to the letter...To see children happy and getting along with one another is a greater thrill to a father than seeing their performance on dos and don'ts."[3]
—Dan DeHaan

"If we want the poor to see Christ in us, we must first see Christ in the poor."[5]
—Mother Teresa

22. Check times you feel that God withholds His compassions.

☐ when I fail to pray
☐ when I sin
☐ when I knowingly rebel
☐ when I am unforgiving
☐ when I have a bad attitude
☐ when I am sad
☐ when I am lonely

23. Check times you withhold your compassion from other Christians.

☐ when they fail to pray
☐ when they sin
☐ when they knowingly rebel
☐ when they are unforgiving
☐ when they have a bad attitude
☐ when they are sad
☐ when they are lonely

24. How does verse 14 speak to you?

25. Check all that apply.

☐ Sometimes I have more expectations of myself than God has.
☐ Sometimes I have more expectations of others than God has.
☐ I have difficulty accepting God's compassion toward me.
☐ I have difficulty extending compassion to those I don't think deserve it.
☐ Sometimes I feel like God has little compassion for me because I rarely see it in other Christians.
☐ I think of compassion as an emotion.

DAY 4

In yesterday's passage we read, "Bless the Lord, O my soul...Who crowns you with lovingkindness and compassion" (Ps. 103:2,4). The picture is incomplete if we are only on the receiving end. We will continue to look at God's compassion and how it relates to His compassion in us.

The Lord opens the eyes of the blind; The Lord raises up those who are bowed down; The Lord loves the righteous; The Lord protects the strangers; He supports the fatherless and the widow (Ps. 146:8-9).

Read Matthew 25:31-46.

26. Whom do the sheep represent?

27. Whom do the goats represent?

28. How does Jesus describe the needy in verses 35-36?

29. Whom did the sheep actually help according to verse 40?

30. Have you ever come face to face with Jesus? When?

31. Check "sheep" or "goats" for each truth:

   Promised the blessing of the Father.   ❑ sheep ❑ goats
   Promised eternal punishment.   ❑ sheep ❑ goats
   Unconscious of their goodness.   ❑ sheep ❑ goats
   Unconscious of their neglect.   ❑ sheep ❑ goats

32. Check the significant difference between the sheep and the goats.

   ❑ their words
   ❑ their actions
   ❑ their amount of Bible study
   ❑ their social status

33. When you treat someone nicely, to whom are you being nice?

34. When you hurt someone, whom are you hurting?

35. How would your actions be affected if you saw the face of Jesus in every person?

36. Who are the forgotten or the friendless at your school?

37. What do they need?

   ❑ A hero with whom they would feel honored to be seen.
   ❑ Kindness from someone who wants to ease their conscience.
   ❑ A friend.

38. What have you learned about God's compassion today?

DAY 5

Sometimes we become the object of our own "compassion." It's called self-pity, self-absorption, and so forth. And yes, sometimes our circumstances seem to force us to look inward. We know from digging into the passages in this study so far that God's compassion is indeed available for us. Maybe the issue is that we're just not experiencing it. Today's study helps us see why.

> "If we are God's friends, and come as such to Him, we must prove ourselves the friends of the needy."[6]
> —Andrew Murray

Read Isaiah 58:1-12.

39. Check any of the below that have ever applied to you:

- ❏ I have been depressed.
- ❏ I have been envious of others.
- ❏ I have thought it would be good if I could switch places with another person.
- ❏ I have felt distanced from God.
- ❏ I have felt that my life is out of order.

40. God says that just going through the motions of worship is not enough. What are some actions that accompany superficial worship?

Verse 4

Verse 5

Verse 9

41. What are some actions that accompany true or right worship?

Verse 6

Verse 7

42. Verse 8—What becomes of a person who partakes in true worship?

43. Which column best describes your life right now?

Darkness	Light
Gloom	Sunshine
Weak	Strong
All dried up	Watered garden

If you give yourself to the hungry and satisfy the desire of the afflicted, Then... (v. 10).

It does not say, "Wait until your gloom is gone and your strength returns and then give yourself to the needy and the afflicted." Instead it says to give yourself to the afflicted in the middle of your own affliction; give yourself to the poor in the middle of your own poverty, and so forth. If you do this, you will not have time for self-absorption or self-pity. What an incredible cure for emotional and physical affliction—helping others.

44. Verse 11—Personally describe a spiritually "scorched place."

45. List practical things you can do to return to the "springs of water." (vv. 9-12)

"The poor will never cease to be in the land; therefore I command you, saying, 'You shall freely open your hand to your brother, to your needy and poor in your land'" (Deut. 15:11).

46. What is the difference between compassion that originates in man and the compassion that originates in God?

This week you should know how to share this much of the "God Is Not a Man" Illustration. You should have two verses memorized. You should be able to draw this from memory.

[1]Dietrich Bonhoeffer, *The Cost of Discipleship* (New York: Macmillan Publishing Company, 1963), 224.
[2]Taken from *The God You Can Know* by Dan DeHaan, Moody Press, copyright 1982, 2001), 78. Used with permission.
[3]Ibid, 79.
[4]C. S. Lewis, *The Problem of Pain* (New York: Macmillan Publishing Company, 1962, 1976), 96-97.
[5]Mother Teresa, *In the Heart of the World: Thoughts, Stories & Prayers* (Ann Arbor: Servant Books, 1985), 126.
[6]Andrew Murray, *With Christ In the School of Prayer*, 1978. Used by permission of Whitaker House, 30 Hunt Valley Circle, New Kensington, PA 15068.

God Is Not a Man
(Num. 23:19; 1 Sam. 15:29; 1 Cor. 1:25)

Man   **God**

Willfully hurts. . . . . Lamentations 3:22-23; Psalm 103:8; Matthew 9:36 . . . Compassionate

God Is Not a Man Illustration, David Stephens *Discovering Who He Is*, (Tulsa: D-Vine Focus, 1989), page 1.

THE GRACE OF GOD

SCRIPTURE MEMORY
God Harbors No Grudge
■ Psalm 103:12
■ Isaiah 43:25
■ Micah 7:19

DAY 1

Have you ever been in the checkout line and when the cashier rang up the amount of your purchase, you realized that you didn't have enough money? Someone you've never met or whom you will probably never see again steps up and makes up the difference: undeserved mercy in your time of need. Some of us see the grace of God like that. We have a need, and God steps up to meet that need. This is not a true picture of God's grace.

Or what if you got up to the cashier and discovered that you had no money at all, and the person behind you paid for everything and then sent you on your way without any expectation of repayment. This sounds a lot like the grace of God, doesn't it? You owe an amount you can't pay, and someone else picks up the tab. But this illustration still doesn't give the complete picture of grace.

Maybe we could see a small hint of God's grace at that checkout line, if the person behind you was someone to whom you owed a lot of money—let's say $850,000,000 and they stepped up behind you noticing that you had no money to pay what you owed the cashier. After they pay for the merchandise, they cancel all previous debt. Then they hand over to you the keys to a new car, the house you desire (completely furnished) and everything you need for life.

For most of us, we only see God's grace as cancelling the debt. After that He goes His way from the supermarket and you go yours. Oh yes, the debt is still covered—eternal life is still yours, but any future blessings are up to you and your performance.

Grace is **G**od's **r**iches **a**t **C**hrist's **e**xpense. Of course there are many people you will come in contact with who are still trying to pay the cashier for something that has already been purchased for them. For today, let's understand grace as it is first experienced in salvation.

What then? Are we better than they? Not at all; for we have already charged that both Jews and Greeks are all under sin; as it is written, "There is none righteous, not even one; There is none who understands, There is none who seeks for God; All have turned aside, together they have become useless; there is none who does good, There is not even one" (Rom. 3:9-12).

Read Ephesians 2:1-9.

1. **How do the following verses remind you that the salvation of God in Christ is undeserving?**

   Verse 1

   Verse 2

   Verse 3

2. **Verse 4—Why does God demonstrate His mercy toward us?**

3. **What has God's grace accomplished for you? (vv. 5-6)**

4. **Verse 7—Who is the channel of God's grace?**

5. **Why is there no place for boasting in regard to the gospel of Jesus Christ? (vv. 8-9)**

"I, even I, am the one who wipes out your transgressions for My own sake; And I will not remember your sins" (Isa. 43:25).

As far as the east is from the west, so far has He removed our transgressions from us (Ps. 103:12).

"Thou hast cast all my sins behind Thy back" (Isa. 38:17).

"My transgression is sealed up in a bag, And Thou dost wrap up my iniquity" (Job 14:17).

6. **According to these verses where are your sins today?**

7. **Sometimes it's hard for me to believe that God could forgive...**

   ❏ the sins I commit today.
   ❏ the sins I committed before I accepted Christ.
   ❏ the sins I do over and over.
   ❏ the sins of the future.

Read Romans 5:20-21.

J. B. Phillips translates this passage like this, "Now we find that the Law keeps slipping into the picture to point the vast extent of sin. Yet, though sin is

Grace is:

**God's
Riches
At
Christ's
Expense.**

"To 'abound' in sin: that is the worst and the most we could or can do. The word *abound* defines the limit of our finite abilities; and although we feel our iniquities [sins] rise over us like a mountain, the mountain, nevertheless, has definable boundaries: it is large, so high, it weighs only this certain amount and no more. But who shall define the limitless grace of God? Its 'much more' plunges our thoughts into infinitude and confounds them there. All thanks be to God for grace abounding."[1]
—A. W. Tozer

shown to be wide and deep, thank God his grace is wider and deeper still! The whole outlook changes—sin used to be the master of men and in the end handed them over to death; now grace is the ruling factor, with its purpose making men right with God and its end the bringing of them to eternal life through Jesus Christ our Lord."[2]

Every bad thing—death, disease, war, and so forth—is a result of sin in the human race. Every good thing comes as a result of God's undeserved mercy, His grace toward us in Christ Jesus.

8. What are some things that you are thankful for?

9. How does it help to know that these things are the reward of God's grace and not a reward of anything you have done?

DAY 2

Jesus said in Matthew 5:3, "Blessed are the poor in spirit, for theirs is the kingdom of heaven." Today we will look at a parable which helps us to understand what Jesus meant by "poor in spirit." We will look at two men—one man who understood his spiritual poverty and one who didn't.

Read Luke 18:9-14.

10. Verse 9—What is indicated as an enemy of grace?

11. In whom and what did the Pharisee place his confidence? (vv. 11-12)

12. What was the difference in the way the tax-gatherer responded as compared to the response of the Pharisee?

13. Verse 14—Why was the tax-gatherer justified and the Pharisee not?

14. Verse 14 says, "he who humbles himself shall be exalted," how is humility related to a person's experiencing God's grace?

15. Sometimes those who have been reared in church and have a strong moral character are hardest to reach with the message of Christ, while those with a history of moral corruption and little church background embrace it with ease. Why do you think this is so?

16. Verse 12—What is the danger of boasting in our own works?

17. **How would a person who boasted in his own works measure the value of other Christians?**

18. **Many of us come to a place in our Christian walk where we want a more tangible way of measuring our Christianity—a way to make us feel spiritual. List some of the ways we do this.**

Maybe you have never made a list but you have a thought about them. Maybe you measure success as a Christian by them. This is what the Pharisees did in the New Testament. They added to God's laws, actually making up new laws that were impossible to keep. They required more than God.

19. **Look at your list again. Do you always do everything you have written here? If not, how can you put that burden on others?**

20. **How should you measure success as a Christian?**

21. **Think of a Christian that you consider to be less committed or faithful because he doesn't do the things you listed. How could you demonstrate grace to this person?**

22. **Write your week 8 memory verse ("Applying the Word").**

DAY 3

"An honest day's work for an honest day's wage." The world tells us that this is what life owes us. As Christians we find this philosophy subtly sweeping us away from the very heart of grace. In the doctrine of grace there is no room for words like "earn" "deserve" and "owe." Maybe it's harder to accept than we would like to admit—that grace is absolutely undeserved. Jesus found Peter and the other disciples a little confused on this matter, too, and so He told them a parable about some laborers in a vineyard.

Read Matthew 19:27-30 and Matthew 20:1-15.

23. **Verse 27—What does Peter seem to think he deserves? Why?**

24. **How does Jesus respond to him? (v. 28)**

25. **What important lesson do we learn about God's grace from verse 29?**

26. **Is the landowner in the parable generous, unfair, or both? Explain.**

27. Why did the landowner hire people so late in the day? (vv. 6-7)

28. What was the response of those first hired to their pay? (v. 11)

29. How do you think those hired last responded to their pay?

30. Which of the workers do you relate to most? Explain.

31. What aspects of grace do you see in this parable?

32. Check all that apply. Sometimes I:

❑ live with a vague sense of God's disapproval.
❑ hesitate to pray after I have just failed Him.
❑ think His grace makes up the difference between the best I can do and what He expects from me.
❑ feel I deserve answered prayer because I have worked hard or sacrificed.
❑ feel more confident before Him if I've been faithful with prayer, quiet time, witnessing, and so forth.
❑ don't see myself as completely blameless in His eyes.
❑ don't experience consistent peace and joy in my Christian life.
❑ don't believe He likes me.
❑ can think of someone I look down upon.
❑ shy away from asking for things because I think it annoys Him.
❑ fear that the day may not go as well when I miss my quiet time.
❑ I've been called into His service because of my worthiness or qualifications.

If you checked any of the above, you do not have a right concept of grace.

Read 2 Samuel 9:1-13.

33. How does Mephibosheth respond to David's generosity in verse 8?

Jonathan's loyal friendship with David (1 Sam. 18:1,3) "earned" Mephibosheth's seat at David's table. Just as we are elevated to the status as God's children for Christ's sake, we become His children when we are born again.

34. What else does his father's friendship earn Mephibosheth? (vv. 7,9,10)

35. Besides salvation what has Christ earned for you?

This story is a beautiful illustration of God's grace toward us. Let's think of the characters in the story this way:

David represents God
Jonathan represents Christ
Mephibosheth represents us (crippled and lame)
The king's table (v. 7) represents salvation
Mephibosheth's lame feet represent our need for dependence

36. When do you feel the most confident in praying to God?

37. How does this reflect a healthy or unhealthy concept of His grace?

You will never deserve to receive a blessing from God, to have any prayer answered, to find a perfect mate, to have all of your needs met in this life or even to be used by God for His glory. But grace is not an issue of deserving. If you deserved it, it would not be grace.

38. What was Mephibosheth's status at the king's table? (vv. 7,10,11,13)

"As if to emphasize the special privilege of Mephibosheth, the inspired writer mentions four times in one short chapter that Mephibosheth ate at the king's table... the account both begins and ends with the statement that Mephibosheth was crippled in both feet. Mephibosheth never got over his crippled condition. He never got to the place where he could leave the king's table and make it on his own. And neither do we."[5]

DAY 5

We will wrap up this week by looking at the ministry of grace in the second and third person's of the Godhead—Jesus, the Son and the Holy Spirit.

39. Read 2 Corinthians 8:9. Why is Jesus the living demonstration of God's grace?

40. What does it mean that he was rich and that he became poor?

41. How rich are you?

42. Read 2 Corinthians 9:8. This week has focused on how God's grace is demonstrated to us through Jesus Christ. This verse shows how the ministry of the Holy Spirit demonstrates His grace through us. What does it say?

43. What are some things God has told you to do? Write them below.

> "Every faculty you have, your power of thinking or of moving your limbs from moment to moment, is given you by God. If you devoted every moment of your whole life exclusively to His service you could not give Him anything that was not in a sense His own already. So that when we talk of a man doing anything for God or giving anything to God, I will tell you what it is really like. It is like a small child going to its father and saying, 'Daddy, give me sixpence to buy you a birthday present.' Of course, the father does, and he is pleased with the child's present. It is all very nice and proper, but only an idiot would think that the father is sixpence to the good on the transaction."[6]
> —C. S. Lewis

44. According to 2 Corinthians 9:8, how are you able to accomplish these things and anything God tells you to do?

45. List personal weaknesses (sin, physical limitations, etc.).

46. Read 2 Corinthians 12:9. How do you think God responds to you in regard to these weaknesses?

[1] A. W. Tozer, *The Knowledge of the Holy* (San Francisco: Harper & Row, Publishers, Inc., 1961), 103.

[2] Reprinted with permission of Macmillan Publishing Co., Inc. from J. B. Phillips: *The New Testament in Modern English*, Revised Edition. © J. B. Phillips 1958, 1960, 1972).

[3] Oswald Chambers, *My Utmost for His Highest* (Westwood: Barbour and Company, Inc., 1935, 1963], 111.

[4] Jerry White, *Honesty, Morality & Conscience* (Colorado Springs: NavPress, 1979), 175.

[5] Jerry Bridges, *Transforming Grace Living Confidently in God's Unfailing Love* (Colorado Springs: NavPress, 1991], 24.

[6] *Mere Christianity* by C. S. Lewis copyright © C. S. Lewis Pte. Ltd. 1942, 1943, 1945, 1944, 1952. Extract reprinted by permission.

This week you should know how to share this much of the "God Is Not a Man" Illustration. You should have your three verses memorized. You should be able to draw this much on a piece of paper from memory.

God Is Not a Man
(Num. 23:19; 1 Sam. 15:29; 1 Cor. 1:25)

Man   **God**

Willfully hurts. . . . . Lamentations 3:22-23; Psalm 103:8; Matthew 9:36 . . . Compassionate

Remembers failures . . . . Isaiah 43:25; Psalm 103:12; Micah 7:19 . . . . Harbors no grudge

God Is Not a Man Illustration, David Stephens *Discovering Who He Is*, (Tulsa: D-Vine Focus, 1989), page 1.

WEEK 11
THE SOVEREIGNTY OF GOD

DAY 1

The fact that God is sovereign means that, "He is under no external restraint whatsoever. He is the Supreme Dispenser of all events. All forms of existence are within the scope of His dominion ... God has seen fit to create beings with the power of choice between good and evil. He rules over them in justice and wisdom and grace"[1]

1. Next to each verse write what it says about God.

Deuteronomy 10:17

Job 36:5

Psalm 50:1

Psalm 66:7

Psalm 93:1

Psalm 103:19

Isaiah 40:8,28

Daniel 4:35

Revelation 11:17

2. After reading these verses, write what "God is sovereign" means.

DAY 2

Read Romans 9:6-26.

3. What makes you a citizen of a particular country?

Paul begins this passage by confronting the notions of the Jews that their position with God was based upon (1) their birth, their Jewish heritage beginning with Abraham and his son Isaac; and (2) their deeds.

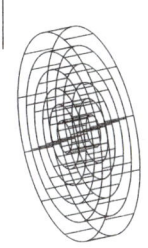

Paul establishes the truth that there is a "new Israel" an "Israel within the Israel." He says, "They are not all Israel who are descended from Israel (v. 6)."

4. Abraham had two sons, Isaac and Ishmael. Whose descendants were the children of the promise? (vv. 7-8)

Isaac	Ishmael
Father–Abraham	Father–Abraham
Mother–**Sarah**	Mother–**Hagar**

A Jew would place his faith in his heritage. Since Abraham was the father of both Ishmael and Isaac, would that mean the chosen descendants were based upon Sarah, placing God under a sense of obligation to make everyone who descended from Isaac a "child of the promise"? No. If God is under obligation then there is no grace. Paul further establishes this in verses 10-13.

5. In verse 10 how many mothers are mentioned? How many sons? Name those mentioned. Who is the father?

Two sons from the same father and mother. The obligation would be for the older son to rule over the younger, but obligation leaves no room for grace.

6. So what did God do? (vv. 11-12)

Jacob	Esau
Father–**Isaac**	Father–**Isaac**
Mother–**Rebekah**	Mother–**Rebekah**

7. Verse 13—"Jacob I loved, but Esau I hated." Jacob was chosen and Esau was not. Upon what basis was Jacob chosen?

8. What was not the basis for his being chosen?

9. With obligation removed and God's sovereignty established, God is then freed to do what? (vv. 15-16)

10. Write your week 9 memory verse ("The Compassion of God").

11. Why is it significant that the God who is in control of all things is as compassionate as He is sovereign?

When Pharaoh saw that there was relief, he hardened his heart and did not listen to them, as the Lord had said (Ex. 8:15).

Pharaoh hardened his heart this time also, and he did not let the people go (Ex. 8:32).

12. Romans 9:17—What was the purpose of Pharaoh's position?

13. Would you agree or disagree that this is also the purpose of every believer? Explain.

He who does wrong will receive the consequences of the wrong which he has done, and that without partiality (Col. 3:25).

In God's sovereignty, He uses both the believer and the non-believer to accomplish His purpose. He deals in justice with the non-believer. He deals in mercy with the believer. Both bring fear and awe to His name.

God is like the sun and some people are like clay or chocolate. In response to Him, some people are hardened and some are softened.

14. How does Paul illustrate God's sovereignty? (vv. 20-21)

15. Verse 22—What are God's two ways to deal with a vessel of wrath?

16. Why do we deserve to be a vessel of wrath?

17. When did you personally become a vessel of mercy?

18. Since God is sovereign and not under obligation to make a person His child because of his birth or deeds, what is He able to do? (vv. 24-26)

19. Why are you a descendant of the "new Israel"?

DAY 3

In the exercise of God's supremacy, He must do right. Whatever He does must be consistent with His nature. Before the creation of the world, God's sovereignty chose to place each of His creatures on a footing which seemed good in His sight. The following illustrates these truths. (based upon the chapter *The Sovereignty of God*,[3] from *The Attributes of God*, Arthur W. Pink)

C. S. Lewis says something like this: A non-believer may bring a person to God, but only a believer can bring God to a person.

Creature	Footing	Explanation
Adam	Conditional	God chose to set him in Eden so that he stood or fell on the condition of whether or not he was obedient to His maker.
Israel	Conditional	Under a covenant of works, God would bless them as a nation on the condition that they observed His laws.
Christ	Conditional	Jesus was made in the likeness of sinful flesh. He was to honor and magnify the law. He was to bear all the sins of the people in His own body. He was to make full atonement for them. He was to endure the wrath of God poured out upon Him. He was to die and be buried.

While the creatures failed, Jesus did not and could not fail. And upon fulfilling these conditions, He was promised to be the first-born among many brethren. He was to have a people who would share His glory.

Creature	Footing	Explanation
The Elect	Unconditional	Because Christ took our place, we now share His. His life is ours. His standing before God is ours. There is not a single condition for us to meet because He met them all on our behalf.

In His sovereignty, God also predetermined to "limit" Himself in some areas. The most obvious example of this is in the incarnation—when God came to earth. Though He was fully divine, He was also fully human, so that He experienced the same limitations as man—fatigue, hunger, thirst, and so forth.

When God predetermined Adam's standing, He could not go back on what He had predetermined to be right. God is unchangeable. To change His mind would be inconsistent with His character. And God can never contradict His nature. So, God could not say, "Well, we'll just let Adam off the hook this time." The condition had already been determined. And Adam fell.

God says, "First of all, then, I urge that entreaties and prayers, petitions and thanksgivings, be made on behalf of all men, for kings and all who are in authority, in order that we may lead a tranquil and quiet life in all godliness and dignity" (1 Tim. 2:1-2). He could "make" us live a quiet and godly life. But in His sovereignty, He has chosen to limit Himself on the basis of the prayers of His people.

20. If our nation is not producing a "tranquil and quiet life" is it safe to assume that we are not praying for "all who are in authority"?

And is this not also true in regard to the salvation of the lost, and the salvation of the world (Col. 4:3)? God has predetermined to move according to the prayers of His people.

Read Acts 17:24-31.

21. What do these verses say about God? (vv. 24-25)

22. Verse 26—What are God's boundaries for you?

23. Verse 27—Since a person doesn't control his own times or boundaries what will this cause him to do?

By now you may be thinking, *Where does the freedom of choice come in to all of this?* It may seem contradictory that man has the freedom of choice if God is sovereign—in control of all things. For a person to make a decision, even a wrong one, he does not go against the Sovereignty of God, but fulfills it. In His sovereignty, God decided not which choice man should make but that he should be free to make it.

These two irreconcilable truths, man's freedom of choice and the sovereignty of God, that co-exist, so to speak, are illustrated by A. W. Tozer:

"An ocean liner leaves New York bound for Liverpool. Its destination has been determined by proper authorities. Nothing can change it. This is at least a faint picture of sovereignty."

"On board the liner are several scores of passengers. These are not in chains, neither are their activities determined for them by decree. They are completely free to move about as they will. They eat, sleep, play, lounge about on the deck, read, talk, altogether as they please; but all the while the great liner is carrying them steadily onward toward a predetermined port."[5]

24. In God's sovereignty, what else has been determined? (v. 31)

DAY 4

Read 1 Chronicles 29:10-16.

"Thou dost exalt Thyself as head over all" (v. 11).

25. Verse 11—What are the specific things mentioned in which the Lord is the determining factor?

26. Verse 12—What are other specifics that fall under God's sovereignty?

Sometimes we look at the honor and riches of others and think some are deserving and some are not. The truth is, what we deserve is death (Rom. 6:23). Anything we have or own is a result of God's grace.

> "God created things which had free will. That means creatures which can go either wrong or right... If a thing is free to be good it is also free to be bad... Why, then, did God give them free will? Because free will, though it makes evil possible, is also the only thing that makes possible any love or goodness or joy worth having."[4]
> —C. S. Lewis

27. Complete the exercise based upon 1 Chronicles 29:12.

If God can...	Then He can also...
make us rich	make us poor
give honor	
give power and might	
establish greatness	
strengthen	

28. What do verses 14-16 say to further establish the truth that everything comes from God and that He rules over all?

DAY 5

Read Genesis 37:1-17.

The following is a brief account of Joseph's life in Egypt. The events once again demonstrate God's sovereignty.

Genesis 37:20—Joseph's brothers throw him in a pit to die then sell him to some Midianite traders as a slave.
Genesis 37:29-35—His brothers deceive their father Jacob into believing Joseph is dead.
Genesis 37:36—Joseph is sold to Potiphar, Pharaoh's officer in Egypt.
Genesis 39:1-6—God gives Joseph favor with Potiphar. He is put in charge of everything.
Genesis 39:7-20—Potiphar's wife tries to seduce him, but he refuses her. She lies and says he tried to seduce her. Potiphar throws him in jail.
Genesis 39:21—God gives Joseph favor with the jailer.
Genesis 40:1-23—Joseph rightly interprets the dreams of his prison mates, the chief cupbearer, and the chief baker.
Genesis 41:1-36—Two years pass. Joseph interprets the dream of Pharaoh, predicting seven years abundance followed by seven years of famine.
Genesis 41:37-57—Pharaoh exalts Joseph to the highest position in Egypt, second only to himself. As predicted seven years of abundance were seen in the land in which Joseph gathered food in preparation for the seven years of famine. Everyone had to come to Egypt for food.

Read Genesis 42:1-38.

Joseph's brothers make their second journey to Egypt (Gen. 43:1-15).

Read Genesis 43:16-34; 44:1-34; 45:1-18.

29. Which of the circumstances in Joseph's life could have caused him to wonder if God had forgotten him?

30. What were Joseph's thoughts on what happened ? (Gen. 45:5-8)

Later, after Joseph learned of his father's death, he tells his brothers, *"As for you, you meant evil against me, but God meant it for good in order to bring about this present result, to preserve many people alive"* (Gen. 50:20).

We know that God causes all things to work together for good to those who love God, to those who are called according to His purpose (Rom. 8:28).

31. God took a tragic event and used it to preserve a nation. Considering Romans 8:28, how does God's sovereignty rule in your life?

32. Do you remember how old Joseph was when all of this started? (Gen. 37:2) How does this encourage you, as a teenager, in your walk with the Lord?

> "So often we blame people, wring our hands over evil, blast life for what it's doing to us. Growth in grace comes when we accept that nothing can happen without God's permission. With that tough fiber in our thinking, we can ask God for power and intervention in what he has either allowed or arranged."[6]
> —Lloyd John Ogilvie

---

[1]Taken from *The New Unger's Bible Dictionary* by Merrill F. Unger, Moody Press © 1957, 1961, 1966). Used by permission.
[2]Elisabeth Elliot, *Discipline: The Glad Surrender*, Fleming H. Revell, a division of Baker Book House Company, 1982, 33.
[3]Arthur W. Pink, *The Attributes of God* (Swengel: Reiner Publications, 1968), 28-30.
[4]*Mere Christianity* by C. S. Lewis copyright © C. S. Lewis Pte. Ltd. 1942, 1943, 1944, 1952. Extract reprinted by permission.
[5]A. W. Tozer, *The Knowledge of the Holy* (Lincoln: Back to the Bible Broadcast, 1961), 118.
[6]*Lord of the Impossible*, Lloyd John Ogilvie, 1984, Abingdon Press. Used by permission.

WEEK 12
AUTHORITY

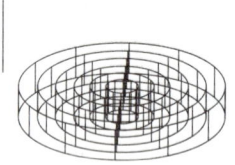

DAY 1

In the Book of Judges, one underlying truth continually emerges. "In those days there was no king in Israel; every man did what was right in his own eyes" (Judg. 21:25. See also Judg. 17:6; 18:1; 19:1.)

The New Ungers Bible Dictionary says, "Each tribe took thought for itself how best to secure and maintain an adequate territory, so that separate interests of all sorts soon became prevalent and regard for the general welfare was more and more forgotten. This separation of the parts of the nation was aided by the early disunion and jealousies of the several tribes, no one of which held preeminence. The consequences of this internal discord were so threatening that it became a grave question whether the nation would be able to hold even the soil on which its peculiar religion and culture were to attain their full development."[1]

1. What would the world be like if there was no authority to which to be held accountable?

2. Write your week 11 memory verse ("God's Sovereignty").

There is a basic relationship between power and authority. Without power there is no authority. Last week, we discovered that since God has total control, He is the head over all authority. God is sovereign. He is in control. His sovereignty is the basis for His authority.

Jesus taught, affirmed, and modeled submission to authority. Today, as we focus on passages from the gospels, we will observe Jesus' life in relationship to authority, and lay the foundation for this study and its over-all topic.

3. Matthew 28:18—What is Jesus' relationship to authority?

Look at how John 8:28-29 characterizes His relationship to authority: Jesus therefore said, "'When you lift up the Son of Man, then you will know that I am He, and I do nothing on My own initiative, but I speak these things as the Father taught Me. And He who sent Me is with Me; He has not left Me alone, for I always do the things that are pleasing to Him."

If all authority has been given to Jesus, why did He only do the things that the Father wanted Him to do? Jesus voluntarily positioned Himself under God while He was here on earth. He accepted this order of authority.

4. **According to Luke 9:1-2 who gave authority to the disciples? Over what had they been given authority?**

5. **According to John 19:10-11 what was Pilate's concept of authority?**

6. **Yet, what does Jesus make perfectly clear? (v. 11)**

Read Matthew 8:5-10.

7. **Why did the Centurion come to Jesus ? (vv. 5-6)**

8. **Verse 7—What does Jesus say?**

9. **Verse 9—What did the Centurion realize about his own submission to authority? What did he realize about the soldier's submission to authority?**

10. **Verse 10—What was Jesus' response to the Centurion's answer?**

Jesus marveled at his faith because the Centurion realized that the authority he had was a result of the authority to which he submitted himself. So, we begin to understand one of the great principles of authority, that the *more a person submits to Jesus, the more authority he/she has in this life.* The world communicates just the opposite—that power and authority are the result of rebelliousness and control. This is a lie. The more a person submits, the more authority he/she will have from God.

DAY 2

The word *submit* may have a negative connotation by today's standards. It conjures up images of suppressed freedom. The biblical principles of authority and submission, however, actually lead us into a life of joy and liberty. Today's passages examine the roles of authority as ordained by God, and the results as we respond to that authority.

Read Ephesians 5:22-33 and 6:1-9.

11. **What are the rewards of submitting to authority? (See Eph. 5:27; 6:3,8.)**

12. **Why are the principles in these verses rejected by the world?**

13. What responsibility has God given to the wife? (See Eph. 5:22,24,33.)

14. What responsibility has God given the husband? (See Eph. 5:23,25,28,31,33)

15. How is the husband to love his wife?

16. What significance do you see in Paul's comparing the relationship between husband and wife with Christ and the church?

17. Verse 30—As Christians, why should we make submission to earthly authority a priority?

Read Ephesians 6:1-9.

18. What's the difference between honoring and obeying your parents?

19. Verse 3—What is promised to the person who submits to parental authority?

20. How might a person abuse his position of authority? (vv. 4,9)

21. What principles could you apply to a job situation ? (vv. 5-9)

22. Verse 7—What should be the underlying motive of your work?

23. How could this perspective make a difficult employer easier to endure?

24. How might it help you when you are demanded to compromise Christ's lordship of your life?

Servants, be submissive to your masters with all respect, not only to those who are good and gentle, but also to those who are unreasonable (1 Pet. 2:18).

"No authority can force you to violate your convictions and cause you to sin. If those in authority force an unethical situation, resignation is the answer. When confronted with a decision, refuse immediately. Don't think it over or give long explanations. It is risky, but have faith in God, trusting Him to protect you."[2]

DAY 3

In today's passages we will discover the impact of authority and our response to it in relation to the well-being of the church.

Read 1 Thessalonians 5:12-13.

25. List people who "have charge over you in the Lord."

26. With these specific people in mind, list ways you can show each your appreciation through...

words

actions

attitudes

To esteem them very highly does not mean to put them on a pedestal. In fact, you will help them more by accepting that they are human and that a position of spiritual leadership brings direct and continual attack from the enemy—an enemy who fights dirty and who is not above using even you (without your even knowing it!) to bring discouragement and defeat.

27. Why is it important to recognize that those with a position of spiritual authority have been ordained by God?

28. Why is it important to recognize God as the Ultimate Authority on all spiritual matters?

Oswald Chambers writes, "Our Lord never insists on having authority; He never says—Thou shalt. He leaves us perfectly free—so free that we can spit in His face, as men did; so free that we can put Him to death, as men did; and He will never say a word. But when His life has been created in me by His Redemption, I instantly recognize His right to absolute authority over me... It is only the unworthy in me that refuses to bow down to the worthy. If when I meet a man who is more holy than myself, I do not recognize his worthiness and obey what comes through him, it is a revelation of the unworthy in me. God educates us by means of people who are a little better than we are, not intellectually but 'holily,' until we get under the domination of the Lord Himself, and then the whole attitude of the life is one of obedience to Him."[3]

He answered and said, "Every plant which My heavenly Father did not plant shall be rooted up" (Matt. 15:13).

29. If a person's position of spiritual authority has not been God-ordained, what will happen to him?

Read Hebrews 13:17.

30. List responsibilities for spiritual leaders and those being led.

31. If you were in a position of spiritual authority, what could those under your leadership do to make it a joyful experience for you?

"He who receives a prophet in the name of a prophet shall receive a prophet's reward; and he who receives a righteous man in the name of a righteous man shall receive a righteous man's reward" (Matt. 10:41).

When you share in the ministry of another, you share in their reward. Their success is your success. The ultimate purpose of submitting to each other in love is to bring glory and honor to God, the Father.

DAY 4

Our attitude toward authority reveals a lot about our attitude toward God. Today's passage looks specifically at our relationship to government authority and the blessings or consequences that result.

Read Romans 13:1-7.

32. What important truth does verse 1 teach us about authority?

33. Verse 2—When a person rebels against authority who is he actually rebelling against?

"You shall not curse God, nor curse a ruler of your people" (Ex. 22:28).

34. What are the consequences of resisting authority? (vv. 2,4)

35. What are the blessings of submitting to authority? (vv. 3,5)

36. If God is our Ultimate Authority, why does Paul give so much attention to the way we submit to governing authorities, the laws they enforce (vv. 1,5-7), and other earthly authority?

Submit yourselves for the Lord's sake to every human institution, whether to a king as the one in authority, ... For such is the will of God that by doing right you may silence the ignorance of foolish men (1 Pet. 2:13,15).

37. How does your response to authority affect your witness for Christ?

38. List names of people who have governmental authority over you. Pray for them as you write their names.

DAY 5

Today we will learn from the example of Daniel and how his submission to even the ungodly authority in his life brought glory and honor to God.

Read Daniel 6:1-28.

39. What impresses you about the way Daniel responds to Darius? (v. 21)

40. What impresses you about his loyalty toward God? (vv. 10-11)

41. How had God given Daniel favor with the king? (vv. 3,14,18,19,23)

42. How was God glorified in Daniel's submission to Him? (vv. 16,26-27)

43. What can you learn from Daniel's life in regard to authority?

---

[1] Taken from *The New Unger's Bible Dictionary* by Merrill F. Unger, Moody Press, 1957, 1961, 1966).Used with permission.
[2] Jerry White, *Honesty, Morality and Conscience* (Colorado Springs: NavPress, 1978), 92.
[3] Oswald Chambers, *My Utmost For His Highest* (Westwood: Barbour and Company, Inc., 1935,1963), 145-146.

WEEK 13
PRAYER

SCRIPTURE MEMORY
Prayer
- Philippians 4:6
- Colossians 4:2
- James 5:16

He who planted the ear, does He not hear? (Ps. 94:9).

DAY 1

1. Write your own concept or definition of prayer.

2. How have you struggled in the area of prayer?

Let us therefore draw near with confidence to the throne of grace, that we may receive mercy and may find grace to help in time of need (Heb. 4:16).

If you are like a lot of people, "confident" is hardly the word to describe the way you approach the Father in prayer. Maybe you feel that your needs are too small and that God is too big. Or that your needs are too big and God is too small. Or perhaps you listen to a voice which says things like, "How can you talk to God when you do such bad things?" Have you ever listened to that one? Wise up to it next time. It's the voice that is still trying to convince you that you come to God on your own merit. You don't. You come to God on Christ's merit. How much "confidence" do you think Jesus has in approaching God? That's how much confidence you can have, too.

3. Write your week 2 memory verse ("Fellowship With God").

4. What part does prayer have in your fellowship with Him?

This week we will look at the five parts of prayer: Adoration, Confession, Thanksgiving, Supplication, and Intercession.

Adoration—Praising and worshiping God for who He is.

Read Psalm 145:1-21.

I will praise Thy name forever and ever (Ps. 145:2).

5. Why is God worthy of David's adoration?

6. **Prayer does not have to be spoken. It can be expressed in song. Write a favorite praise chorus or verse that expresses adoration to God.**

7. **Write your week 6 ("God Is Not a Man"), week 9 ("The Compassion of God"), or week 11 ("God's Sovereignty") memory verse.**

8. **Take time now to praise God. Record your thoughts below.**

9. **What does praising God do for the person who prays? (vv. 18-19)**

10. **Why do you think it is the tendency for many to skip over the adoration part of praying?**

DAY 2

Confession—Acknowledging specific sins and claiming God's forgiveness.

Elisabeth Elliott writes, "Sometimes it happens that I can think of nothing that needs confessing. This is usually a sign that I'm not paying attention. I need to read the Bible. If I read it with prayer that the Holy Spirit will open my eyes to this need, I soon remember things done that ought not to have been done and things undone that ought to have been done."[2]

11. **List what each Scripture reveals about sin.**

	Results of Holding on to Sin	Results of Confessing Sin
Proverbs 28:13		
Psalm 32:3-4		
Psalm 32:5		
Psalm 66:18		
1 John 1:9		

Read Matthew 6:14-15.

12. **What else hinders our prayers from accomplishing much?**

13. **Who does the Lord bring to mind as you meditate on these verses?**

14. **What does this motivate you to do?**

"Poverty-stricken as the Church is today in many things, she is most stricken here, in the place of prayer. We have many organizers, but few agonizers; many players and payers, few pray-ers; many singers, few clingers; lots of pastors, few wrestlers; many fears, few tears; much fashion, little passion; many interferers, few intercessors; many writers, but few fighters. Failing here, we fail everywhere."[1]
—Leonard Ravenhill

15. Ask the Lord to bring to mind specific sins. List them below.

16. Write your week 10 memory verse ("God Harbors No Grudge").

17. What promise does this hold for you in regard to the sins you listed?

18. Thank the Lord for His mercy, grace, and forgiveness. Record your thoughts below.

Thanksgiving—Thanking God for His blessings and for the trials that strengthen our character.

Read Psalm 30:1-12.

19. Why is David thankful?

20. List blessings for which you are thankful.

21. List hardships which burden you.

22. How can you be thankful for these things?

In everything give thanks for this is God's will for you in Christ Jesus (1 Thess. 5:18).

23. Thank God for blessings and hardships. Record your thoughts below.

24. Psalm 30:11—How does expressing thankfulness to God impact the one who prays?

DAY 3

Supplication—Earnestly and humbly laying your requests before God.

Read Matthew 7:7-11.

25. What is the purpose of asking, seeking, and knocking?

26. How is prayer the means of asking, seeking, and knocking?

27. How do you respond when God grants you what you wish after you've prayed for it?

28. How do you respond when He doesn't?

29. What do these two answers reveal about your concept of God?

30. What does Jesus reveal about God in verses 9-11?

Dietrich Bonhoeffer writes, "The right way to approach God is to stretch out our hands and ask of One who we know has the heart of a Father."[4]

31. Why would an earthly father say "no" to something for which the child requested?

32. Why might God not always grant what His children request?

33. What prayers are always guaranteed a positive response according to John 14:13; 15:7; James 1:5; 1 John 5:14-15?

34. What does Matthew 6:9-13 reveal as acceptable when praying?

35. Why is it important to know what is on God's heart when you pray?

36. List several things which you want to receive from God.

37. Next to each request write a "G" for God-centered requests, an "S" for self-centered requests, and a "U" if you are unsure.

38. How does James 1:5 help you with the unsure requests?

39. According to Philippians 4:6-7 how else does a person benefit from the prayer of supplication?

40. Talk to God about your list above. When you're finished, record your thoughts below.

"True prayer does not depend either on the individual or the whole body of the faithful, but solely upon the knowledge that our heavenly Father knows our needs. That makes God the sole object of our prayers, and frees us from a false confidence in our own prayerful efforts."[3]
—Dietrich Bonhoeffer

DAY 4

> "Live as a child of God, then you will be able to pray as a child, and as a child you will most assuredly be heard."[5]
> —Andrew Murray

Intercession—Praying, or petitioning, on behalf of another person.

41. How do the following verses instruct us to pray for others?

Matthew 5:44

Ephesians 6:18

Colossians 1:9

Colossians 4:3

1 Timothy 2:1

James 5:16

42. Many of Jesus recorded prayers were prayers of intercession. What does He ask in behalf of the disciples in the following verses?

Luke 22:31-32

John 17:15,17

John 17:20-21

Hence, also, He is able to save forever those who draw near to God through Him, since He always lives to make intercession for them (Heb. 7:25).

43. How is Jesus praying for you? (See question 42.)

44. According to Matthew 26:41 and Luke 22:40 what does Jesus instruct us to pray for?

Max Lucado writes, "Prayer isn't telling God anything new. There is not a sinner nor a saint who would surprise him. What prayer does is invite God to walk the shadowy pathways of life with us. Prayer is asking God to watch ahead for falling trees and tumbling boulders and to bring up the rear, guarding our backside from the poison darts of the devil."[6]

45. Ask the Lord to reveal people for whom you can pray. Write their names in the margin. Pray for your Christian friends the way Jesus prayed for His disciples. When you are through record your thoughts.

DAY 5

46. What specific times of the day can be set aside for prayer?

Psalm 5:3

Psalm 55:17

Psalm 63:6

Luke 6:12

Pray without ceasing (1 Thess. 5:17).

47. When should you pray?

It seems that this is another part of prayer that becomes more of a burden rather than an encouragement. We get in our minds that to be really serious about prayer we must spend no less than two or three hours on our knees. There will be times in your life when God may call you to do this. But the majority of prayers in the Bible are really rather short. Think of the Psalms—these are some of the most beautiful writings in the Scripture. Remember how Christ Himself instructed us to pray. Give the burden of praying to the Lord. Allow Him to lead you in how and what to pray each time.

Charles Swindoll writes, "Prayer was never intended to make us feel guilty. It was never intended to be a verbal marathon for only the initiated ... no secret-code talk for the clergy or a public display of piety. None of that. Real prayer—the kind of prayer Jesus mentioned and modeled—is realistic, spontaneous, down-to-earth communication with the living Lord that results in a relief of personal anxiety and a calm assurance that our God is in full control of our circumstances."[8]

Elisabeth Elliot writes, "Don't try to sit or kneel in one position for too long. Stand up to pray, walk around, go outdoors and pray as you walk. If it is not possible to pray aloud without attracting attention, pray in a whisper."[9]

"When you pray, go into your inner room, and when you have shut your door, pray to your Father who is in secret, and your Father who sees in secret will repay you" (Matt. 6:6).

48. What does this verse say about the hidden nature of prayer?

49. How is this possible even in a room full of people?

"I'm afraid many of us pray with the goal of talking God into things rather than trying to discover His will. Consequently, we never hear from Him. Jesus understood the importance of neutrality."[7]
—Charles Stanley

> **"The secret of praying is praying in secret. A sinning man will stop praying, and a praying man will stop sinning."[10]**
> —Leonard Ravenhill

Oswald Chambers writes, "Swing the door wide open and pray to your Father in secret, and every public thing will be stamped with the presence of God."[11]

50. Write below the one thing from this week's study that has been most encouraging to you in regard to your prayer life. Record any commitments you have made.

[1] Used with permission from *Why Revival Tarries*, by Leonard Ravenhill, © 1959 Bethany House Publishers.

[2] *Trusting God in a Twisted World*, Elisabeth Elliot, Fleming H. Revell, a division of Baker Book House Company, 1989.

[3] Dietrich Bonhoeffer, *The Cost of Discipleship* (New York: Macmillan Publishing Company, 1963), 183.

[4] Ibid, 183.

[5] Andrew Murray, *With Christ In the School of Prayer*, 1978. Used by permission of Whitaker House, 30 Hunt Valley Circle, New Kensington, PA 15068.

[6] Max Lucado, *No Wonder They Call Him the Savior* (Portland: Multnomah, 1986), 152.

[7] Charles Stanley, *The Wonderful Spirit Filled Life* (Nashville: Thomas Nelson, 1992), 176.

[8] *Strengthening Your Grip*, Charles R. Swindoll, 1982, Word Publishing, Nashville, Tennessee. All rights reserved.

[9] Elisabeth Elliot, *Discipline: The Glad Surrender*, Fleming H. Revell Company, a division of Baker Book House Company, 1982.

[10] Ravenhill, *Why Revival Tarries*, 8.

[11] Oswald Chambers, *My Utmost for His Highest* (Westwood: Barbour and Company, Inc., 1935, 1963), 173.

WEEK 14
METHODS OF BIBLE STUDY (JAMES)

This week you will study the Book of James using one or more of the four methods of Bible study introduced in week 8: Ready, Aim, Fire Method; The P's and Q's Method; The Triple S Method; The John 15:5 Method. You may want to refer to week 8 for an example of each method.

SCRIPTURE MEMORY
God Remembers Your Efforts
■ Hebrews 6:10

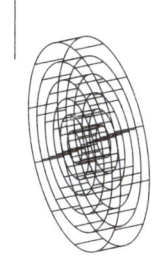

Ready, Aim, Fire Method

Ready—*Bring the principles into focus.* Write points or facts the passage reveals.

Aim—*Finding the target.* What verse stands out to you the most?

Fire—*What does my "target verse" challenge me to do?* How can I put into practice what this verse is saying? What specific commitment do I need to make to live out the truth of this verse?

The P's and Q's Method

P's—*Principles.* Write down the principles the passage teaches.

Q's—*Questions.* Answer the following questions in regard to the principles you discovered in the passage.

   What sin do I need to confess?

   What example do I need to model?

   What command do I need to obey?

Application. Upon answering the questions, what action do I need to take?

The Triple S Method

Standard—State the principle or ideal expressed from one particular verse.

Struggles—How am I not measuring up to this (ideal or principle) in my life?

Strategy—My course of action to change this. How can I apply the Scripture to my problem?

The John 15:5 Method

1. "I am the Vine"—What does this passage reveal about God or Jesus Christ?
2. "You are the branches"—What does this passage reveal about me?
3. "He who abides in Me and I in Him bears much fruit"—What verse from this passage is the Holy Spirit using to prune me so that His fruit can be produced in my life?
4. "For apart from Me you can do nothing"—Pray the following:

Lord, I realize that the first step in applying this truth in my life is to admit that without You I cannot do it. So, I give this to You right now and thank You that no matter what happens, You have taken it. Let me not listen to the voice of the deceiver, who wants me to feel defeated. Let me not trust in my own strength and try to accomplish this in my flesh. But may I place my hope and my trust in You that through Jesus You can accomplish this in me. Amen.

It is important to be specific in your applications. Below are examples of applications for Galatians 6:2, "Bear one another's burdens, and thus fulfill the law of Christ."

Okay: "I will help others more."

Good: "I will be sensitive to someone in need and make myself available to them."

Better: "My mom has had a heavy workload lately so I will bear her burden by helping more around the house."

Best: "God is specifically leading me through this verse to help my mom more around the house since she has had a lot of stress at work. I will do the dishes all week without being asked (whether my brother does his share or not). I will take my brother to soccer practice."

Prove yourselves doers of the word, and not merely hearers who delude themselves (Jas. 1:22).

Ready, Aim, Fire Method
James 1

Ready—*Bring the principles into focus.*

Aim—*Finding the target.*

Fire—*What does my "target verse" challenge me to do?*

DAY 2

The P's and Q's Method
James 2

P's–_Principles_

Q's–_Questions_

What sin do I need to confess?

What example do I need to model?

What command do I need to obey?

Application

DAY 3

The Triple S Method
James 3

Standard

Struggles

Strategy

DAY 4

The John 15:5 Method
James 4

1. "I am the Vine"—What is this saying about God or Jesus Christ?

2. "You are the branches"—What does this passage reveal about me?

3. "He who abides in Me and I in Him bears much fruit"—What verse from this passage is the Holy Spirit using to prune me so that His fruit can be produced in my life?

4. "For apart from Me you can do nothing"—Pray the following.

Lord, I realize that the first step in applying this truth in my life is to admit that without You I cannot do it. So, I give this to You right now and thank You that no matter what happens, You have taken it. Let me not listen to the voice of the deceiver, who wants me to feel defeated. Let me not trust my own strength and try to accomplish this in my flesh. But may I place my hope and my trust in You that through Jesus You can accomplish all things in me. Amen.

Have fun doing your Bible study today. Check one of the following four Bible study methods and apply it to the Scripture passage provided.

❑ **Ready, Aim, Fire Method**
❑ **The P's and Q's Method**
❑ **The Triple S Method**
❑ **The John 15:5 Method**

James 5

This week you should know how to share this much of the "God Is Not a Man" Illustration. You should have your four verses memorized. You should be able to draw this much on a piece of paper.

God Is Not a Man
(Num. 23:19; 1 Sam. 15:29; 1 Cor. 1:25)

Man		God
Willfully hurts.	Lamentations 3:22-23; Psalm 103:8; Matthew 9:36 . . .	Compassionate
Remembers failures	Isaiah 43:25; Psalm 103:12; Micah 7:19	Harbors no grudge
Forgets efforts	Hebrews 6:10	Remembers your efforts

God Is Not a Man Illustration, David Stephens *Discovering Who He Is,* (Tulsa: D-Vine Focus, 1989), page 1.

WEEK 15
GOD IS IMMUTABLE

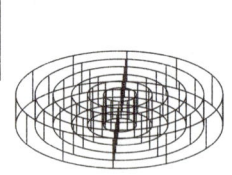

DAY 1

Immutable may be a term with which you are unfamiliar. Some words that mean the opposite of immutable are mutate, mutant, and mutable. These words relate to things which are inconstant or subject to change. Only God is immutable. Since He is immutable, He is unchanging. He is constant. What is the significance of this in your concept of God?

1. To understand God's divine attribute of being immutable, let's look at what is mutable. List changes you have noticed in the last year in:

    Fashion

    Music

    Fads

    Technology

2. What changes do you observe in yourself? (Find an old picture and list the differences you see. How have your friendships changed.)

As a Christian change should occur in your life as you become more like Christ. Consider the following verse.

We all, with unveiled face beholding as in a mirror the glory of the Lord, are being transformed into the same image from glory to glory, just as from the Lord, the Spirit (2 Cor. 3:18).

3. Change can also be negative. Write how you feel when...

    someone whom you admire changes his/her moral standards.

    your closest friend starts spending more time with someone else.

    a family you know experiences divorce.

4. Write your week 6 memory verse ("God Is Not a Man").

5. Next to each verse write how God's immutability is proclaimed.

Psalm 89:33-34

Isaiah 54:10

Malachi 3:6

Hebrews 13:8

James 1:17

6. How do you feel knowing God is immutable in a world that changes everyday?

"In this world where men forget us, change their attitude toward us as their private interests dictate, and revise their opinion of us for the slightest cause, is it not a source of wondrous strength to know that the God with whom we have to do changes not? That His attitude toward us now is the same as it was in eternity past and will be in eternity to come?"

"What peace it brings to the Christian's heart to realize that our Heavenly Father never differs from Himself. In coming to Him at any time we need not wonder whether we shall find Him in a receptive mood. He is always receptive to misery and need, as well as to love and faith. He does not keep office hours nor set aside periods when He will see no one. Neither does He change His mind about anything. Today, this moment, He feels toward His creatures, toward babies, toward the sick, the fallen, the sinful, exactly as He did when He sent His only-begotten Son into the world to die for mankind."[2]

DAY 2

It is impossible to single out one of God's attributes from the rest. When we study His grace, we learn of His love. When we embrace His love, we experience His compassion. And as we try to understand His immutability, we find His eternity is present, as well as His goodness and His sovereignty.

Read Psalm 46:1-11.

7. Write your week 11 memory verse ("God's Sovereignty").

Remember God's sovereignty characterizes His total rulership. God has total control.

8. Verse 5—Why are God's Holy dwelling places immovable?

9. Verse 6—Likewise, what causes the earth to melt?

> "God cannot change for the better. Since He is perfectly holy, He has never been less holy than He is now and can never be holier than He is and has always been. Neither can God change for the worse. Any deterioration within the unspeakably holy nature of God is impossible."[1]
> —A. W. Tozer

10. Who is sovereign over the mutable and the immutable?

11. What do the following verses say about the seemingly immutable things listed below?

    Verse 2–the earth and mountains

    Verse 6–kingdoms

    Verse 9–wars

12. Verse 2—What are the "mountains" in your life that overwhelm you?

13. Maybe these mountains have kept you from resting in the "holy dwelling places of the Most High." (v. 4) What does God have the power to do with these "mountains"?

14. What does verse 5 indicate will happen to the state of your soul when God is your central focus instead of the mountains?

15. Verse 10—How can you experience God's presence moment by moment?

This expression, "Yet once more," denotes the removing of those things which can be shaken, as of created things, in order that those things which cannot be shaken may remain (Heb. 12:27).

Hannah Whitall Smith writes, "Can it be possible that we, who are so easily moved by the things of earth, can arrive at a place where nothing can upset our temper or disturb our calm? Yes it is possible; and the apostle Paul knew it... Everything in Paul's life and experience that could be shaken had been shaken... And we, if we will but let God have His way with us, may come to the same place so that neither the fret and tear of the little things of life, nor its great and heavy trials, can have power to move us from the peace that passeth all understanding."[4]

16. What words in Psalm 46:1,11 establish the immutable presence of God?

DAY 3

Today we will see how God's immutability is confirmed in His promises.

17. How does a person's character affect your ability to trust their word?

18. What might cause a person to break his word?

Read Psalm 105:8-15.

19. How does this passage reveal that God kept His word to Abraham?

20. What motivates God to keep His word?

Read Hebrews 6:13-19.

The promise spoken of in verse 13 is found in Genesis 12:1-3. Now the Lord said to Abram, "Go forth from your country, And from your relatives And from your father's house, To the land which I will show you; And I will make you a great nation, And I will bless you, And make your name great; And so you shall be a blessing; And I will bless those who bless you, And the one who curses you I will curse. And in you all the families of the earth shall be blessed."

Genesis 12:4 says that Abraham was 75 when he left Haren in obedience to the Lord. His son Isaac was not born until Abraham was 100 years old (Gen. 21:5). Twenty-five years elapsed with no hint of a fulfilled promise, then a miracle birth. The Lord tested Abraham's faith again. He commanded him to sacrifice Isaac. Abraham obeyed, but the Lord stopped him and reiterated His promise again in Genesis 22:16-17:

"By Myself I have sworn, declares the Lord, because you have done this thing, and have not withheld your son, your only son, indeed I will greatly bless you, and I will greatly multiply your seed as the stars of the heavens, and as the sand which is on the seashore; and your seed shall possess the gate of their enemies."

21. Verse 16—What does a person do to assure another his word is true?

22. Verse 17—God's promise in itself is enough. So why does He grant additional confirmation?

In verse 18 the "two unchangeable things" are God's promise and His oath.

We may have strong encouragement (v. 18b).

23. Why may we draw encouragement from and place our hope in the promises of God?

24. Review the promises God made to Abraham. He saw only a small portion of these promises fulfilled in his own lifetime and what he did see, came about after much patience and waiting. And yet God's immutable purpose initiated by a promise to Abraham continues today. How is your life a fulfillment of these promises?

25. What is the "hope" spoken of in verses 18-19?

26. Verse 19—What comparisons can you make between an anchor that secures a ship and the hope that secures your soul?

27. What words in verse 19 indicate that this is an immutable hope?

DAY 4

Yesterday, we looked at God's immutability as seen in His purpose and in His promise to Abraham. Today we will see how He is unchanging in His promises toward us and in the law by which He governs our lives.

28. Write your week 7 memory verse ("The Bible, God's Word").

29. What do Matthew 5:18; 24:35 say about God's Word?

30. What is promised in the following verses?

Matthew 28:20

John 14:2-3

1 Corinthians 10:13

Philippians 1:6

Philippians 4:19

1 Peter 5:10

31. Why can you place hope in these and other promises in the Bible even though they were written thousands of years ago?

With a promise, you will nearly always find a condition. The condition to the above promises is that you must be God's child. These are not promises the non-Christian may claim. Yesterday, we looked at how Abraham received the promise with the condition of patiently waiting. In His immutability, God says, "I will... if you will ..."

32. Write the conditions and promises found in the following verses.

	Condition	Promise
Psalm 37:4		
Proverbs 3:5-6		
Isaiah 26:3		
Luke 6:37		
James 4:7		
1 John 1:9		

Sometimes we expect to receive the promises of God without fulfilling the conditions. But God is immutable in regard to both. He is also unchanging in regard to His law.

"...not the smallest letter or stroke shall pass away from the Law"
(Matt. 5:18).

33. Write the world's attitude in regard to:

Divorce

Greed

Pride

Sex

Rebellion

34. Why does the world change its standards in regard to these issues?

35. Write what these verses reveal is God's response to each issue.

Divorce (Mal. 2:16)

Greed (Heb. 13:5)

Pride (1 Pet. 5:5)

Sex (1 Cor. 6:9)

Rebellion (Mal. 3:5)

36. Why do God's standards not change in regard to these issues?

37. Which standards will you choose by which to live your life? Why?

DAY 5

Since God is immutable in His nature we find Him unchanging in all of His attributes. As we shall see in future studies, He is unchanging in His holiness, His love, His faithfulness, and so forth. Today we will look at His immutability in regard to salvation.

Read 1 Peter 1:3-4.

38. Verse 3—Upon what foundation of hope does your spiritual birth rest?

39. When a person dies, he passes along his inheritance to relatives and other beneficiaries. When Christ died and rose from the grave, He passed along His inheritance to His children. How does verse 4 describe this inheritance?

40. Who secures your reservation for eternity even now?

41. What circumstances cause you to doubt your salvation?

Read 2 Timothy 1:12.

He is able to guard what I have entrusted to Him (v. 12e).

42. Have you entrusted your salvation to Christ or to yourself?

43. Why is God able to guard what you've entrusted to Him?

44. Does salvation hinge on God's integrity or yours? Explain.

"Truth does remain because it is stronger than falsehood; goodness remains because it is greater than evil; love remains because it outlives hatred. Men can nail these values to a cross, as they did once nail them to a Cross, but they cannot destroy them, because they are rooted and grounded in the eternal God.[5] —Leonard Griffith

"What does the attribute of God's immutability mean to the Christian? *Comfort.* Someone has a handle on this thing called life. Some things do not change. If ever God loved me, He loves me now. That is what unchangeable means. If ever God forgave me, He forgives me now... If ever God promised me something, He promised me forever... If ever God saved me, He saved me forever."[6]

[1]A. W. Tozer, *The Knowledge of the Holy* (San Francisco: Harper & Row, Publishers, 1961), 55.
[2]Ibid, 59-60.
[3]*God in Man's Experience,* Leonard Griffith, 1968 Word Publishing, Nashville, Tennessee. All rights reserved.
[4]Hannah Whitall Smith, *The God of All Comfort* (New York: Ballantine Books, 1986), 121-122.
[5]*God in Man's Experience,* Leonard Griffith, 78.
[6]Taken from *The God You Can Know* by Dan DeHaan, Moody Press, 1982, 2001. Used with permission.

This week you should know how to share this much of the "God Is Not a Man" Illustration. You should have your five verses memorized. You should be able to draw this much on a piece of paper.

God Is Not a Man
(Num. 23:19; 1 Sam. 15:29; 1 Cor. 1:25)

Man		God
Willfully hurts	Lamentations 3:22-23; Psalm 103:8; Matthew 9:36	Compassionate
Remembers failures	Isaiah 43:25; Psalm 103:12; Micah 7:19	Harbors no grudge
Forgets efforts	Hebrews 6:10	Remembers your efforts
Changes	Hebrews 13:8; James 1:17; Isaiah 54:10	Immutable

God Is Not a Man Illustration, David Stephens *Discovering Who He Is*, (Tulsa: D-Vine Focus, 1989), page 1.

WEEK 16
THE HOLINESS OF GOD

SCRIPTURE MEMORY
Christ Is Sinless
■ Hebrews 4:15
■ Hebrews 7:26
■ 1 John 3:5

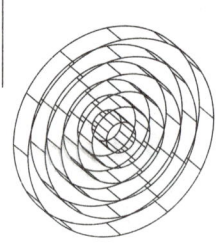

DAY 1

1. Close your eyes and imagine yourself observing a mountain. Write several words that you would use to describe it.

2. Which of these words might you use to describe the presence of God?

Mountains are used figuratively in the Bible to express many things, such as stability, strength, abundance, and even desolation or difficulties. The imagery of mountains in the Bible is also used to reveal who God is. Psalm 36:6 says, "Thy righteousness is like the mountains of God."

We use mountains to describe significant encounters with God. We call them "mountain top" experiences, being spiritually elevated, so to speak. With the peak of the mountain as our point of observation, the valleys below take on their proper perspective.

In relation to the Holiness of God, the mountains teach us the most when we are at their foothills looking up. Today we go to the foothills of Mount Sinai.

Read Exodus 19:9-23.

3. Verse 9—What did the Lord promise Moses?

4. What did the Lord specifically require of the people to prepare for such an encounter?

   Verse 10

   Verse 12

   Verse 15

5. How is the seriousness of coming into the Lord's presence shown? (vv. 12-13,21-22)

The term *holy* in its absolute sense applies only to God—someone set apart and distinct from anything else. Holiness relates to God's perfections in His moral character, but it also includes His "otherness," that which sets Him apart from all He has created.

6. How is God's holiness—His otherness—characterized in relation to the people in verses 12,17,21?

7. What happened on the morning of the third day? (v. 16)

8. When the Lord's presence descended what was the response of...

    the people? (v. 16)

    the mountain? (v. 18)

9. In what forms did He make His presence known?

    Verse 18

    Verse 19

10. What have you learned about the holiness of God?

Our God is a consuming fire (Heb. 12:29).

DAY 2

God's holiness is manifested in all that He is and in all that He does. His holiness also confronts us in all that we are and in all that we do. Yesterday, we looked at mountains as a way of helping us grasp this intangible attribute. Today we join the psalmist in worship at the foothill of "His holy hill."

Read Psalm 99:1-9.

11. How is God characterized in the following verses?

    Verses 1-2—His position

    Verses 4,8—His moral character

    Verses 6-8—His past relations

12. What do "worship at His footstool" (v. 5) and "worship at His holy hill" (v. 9) reveal about the psalmist's concept of his own position in the presence of a holy God?

> "God's holiness is His 'God-ness.' It is His being God in all that it means for Him to be God. To meet God in His holiness, therefore, is to be altogether overwhelmed by the discovery that He is God, and not man."[1]
> —Sinclair B. Ferguson

O Lord our God, Thou didst answer them; Thou wast a forgiving God to them, And yet an avenger of their evil deeds (v. 8).

An *avenger* is someone who punishes a wrong-doer.

13. Where does God direct His forgiveness?

14. Where does He direct His avengement?

15. Why is it impossible for Holy God to take a passive attitude toward sin?

16. Verse 3—What was the reaction of the psalmist to God's holiness?

17. As you keep God's holiness before you, how do you think it will affect the way you live?

Today's passage is Isaiah's account of his own experience of coming into the presence of Holy God. As you read it notice not only the responses of Isaiah and the heavenly beings but also the response of the very building in which this encounter happened.

Read Isaiah 6:1-13.

18. In Isaiah's vision of the presence of God, how does verse 1 describe the position of the Lord?

"Seraphim stood above Him" (v. 2). Seraphim are angels.

19. What did the Seraphim do in the presence of Holy God? (vv. 2-3)

The four living creatures, each one of them having six wings, are full of eyes around and within; and day and night they do not cease to say, "Holy, Holy, Holy, is the Lord God, the Almighty, who was and who is and who is to come" (Rev. 4:8).

Whenever living creatures come into the presence of God, they are confronted at once with His holiness.

20. **What did the presence of God's holiness specifically expose in Isaiah's life? (v. 5)**

Reflecting upon this passage Oswald Chambers writes, "When I get into the presence of God, I do not realize that I am a sinner in an indefinite sense; I realize the concentration of sin in a particular feature of my life... This is always the sign that a man or woman is in the presence of God. There is never any vague sense of sin, but the concentration of sin is some personal particular."[3]

21. **As you come into the presence of God, of what particular sin in your life do you become aware?**

22. **How did the Seraphim minister to Isaiah? (vv. 6-7)**

23. **Verse 8—In dealing with this sin, for what was God preparing Isaiah?**

24. **Verse 9—How did God want to use Isaiah?**

As with Isaiah, could it be that the particular cleansing God wishes to do in your own life is the very area in which He wants to use you. With Isaiah as an example of a willing spirit, meditate on verse 8 in regard to the repentance of sin and the surrender of your life for service.

DAY 4

It is impossible to look directly into the light of the sun for even a moment. Its radiance is so powerful that even a glimpse could cause immediate blindness. But can you think of anything that would result in a person's death if he merely glanced at it?

25. **If you could ask the Lord for your heart's desire right now for what would you ask?**

Read Exodus 33:18-20.

26. **What is the yearning of Moses' heart according to verse 18?**

27. **How did God respond to Moses' request?**

We settle for...	When we could have...
The good things God can do.	A relationship with God, the essence of goodness.
Temporary satisfactions.	A relationship with the Lord, the Alpha and the Omega, the beginning and the end.
Unforgiveness or withdrawal.	God's grace to help in time of need.
Callousness or apathy.	God's unfailing compassion.

28. If God were to suddenly appear right now, what would you do?

29. What does God reveal about Himself to Moses? (v. 20)

30. How does this revelation impact your own concept of God?

Read Exodus 33:21-23.

31. By what condition could Moses see the back of the Lord?

We do not have a high priest who cannot sympathize with our weaknesses, but one who has been tempted in all things as we are, yet without sin (Heb. 4:15).

You know that He appeared in order to take away sins; and in Him there is no sin (1 John 3:5).

32. After reviewing the above verses and studying God's holiness, what new value do you place upon Christ's gift of salvation?

"How can we who are not only guilty but morally filthy possibly be holy in the sight of One whose gaze penetrates our very hearts, who knows our every motive and thought as well as our words and actions? The answer is that because of our union with Christ, God sees *His* holiness as *our* holiness."[5]

By that will, we have been made holy through the sacrifice of the body of Jesus Christ once for all (Heb. 10:10, NIV).[6]

DAY 5

33. Write your week 4 memory verse ("Abiding in Christ").

Jerry Bridges writes, "In one aspect of sanctification you are already holy because Christ's holiness is imputed to you. You have been made perfect forever. In another aspect, you are being made holy day by day through the work of the Holy Spirit impairing Christ's life to you."[7]

We have looked at mountains and what they can teach us in regard to God and our relationship with Him. At Mount Sinai, we saw Him making His presence known through thunder and fire. We understand that His holiness is something that is completely unique to Himself. Just as we stand back and observe the mountains in their majesty and vastness, we can only stand back in breathtaking awe when we consider the holiness of God.

As we yearn for that holiness, we are led to Calvary's mountain. Some call it the Hill of Golgotha. This brings God's holiness to a place where we can receive it—to Christ on the cross.

Read Psalm 24:3-4.

34. Considering the words, "ascend" and "hill," in what direction will a person be headed if he is to stand in "His holy place"?

35. What does this direction mean in a spiritual sense? (v. 4)

36. What "lowlands" in your life do you need to leave behind as you set off for the high country of God?

The Lord God is my strength, And He has made my feet like hinds' feet, And makes me walk on my high places (Hab. 3:19).

37. What happens when you become weary of climbing the mountain of holiness?

38. What happens when you become weary of bringing God's holiness into the canyons of everyday life?

God's purpose in making you holy is not to make you a monument of admiration, but a model of service, as J. Sidlow Baxter writes, "The kind of character-beauty which true holiness begets is not that of elegant marble statuary, charming in profile, graceful in silhouette, yet cold and hard to the touch, voiceless, uncommunicative, and locked up in itself. Any kind of holiness which turns the inner life into a mental monastery, and the outer life into a walled-off enclosure, is not holiness according to Christ. One of the loveliest traits of character engendered by true holiness is a self-forgetting otherism. Instead of a continually in-looking self-culture, there is an out-looking diffusion of goodness to others."[8]

39. Verse 4—When a person is striving after holiness, why might clean hands in a spiritual sense look dirty in a physical sense?

40. Write your week 8 memory verse ("Applying the Word").

[1] *A Heart for God*, Sinclair B. Ferguson, © 1985. Used by Permission of NavPress/Pinon Press. All rights reserved. For Copies call 1-800-366-7788.

[2] J. I. Packer, *Knowing God* (Downers Grove: InterVarsity Press, 1973), 151.

[3] Oswald Chambers, *My Utmost for His Highest* (Westwood: Barbour and Company, Inc., 1935, 1963), 134.

[4] Arthur W. Pink, *Gleanings in Exodus* (Chicago: Moody Press, 1976), 346-347.

[5] Jerry Bridges, *Transforming Grace* (Colorado Springs: NavPress, 1991), 104.

[6] Scripture quotations marked (NIV) are from the Holy Bible, *New International Version*. Copyright © 1973, 1978, 1984 by International Bible Society.

[7] Bridges, *Transforming Grace*, page 103.

[8] J. Sidlow Baxter, *Christian Holiness Restudied and Restated* (Grand Rapids: Zondervan Publishing House, 1977), 162.

This week you should know how to share this much of the "God Is Not a Man" Illustration. You should have your six verses memorized. You should be able to draw this much on a piece of paper.

God Is Not a Man
(Num. 23:19; 1 Sam. 15:29; 1 Cor. 1:25)

Man		God
Willfully hurts	Lamentations 3:22-23; Psalm 103:8; Matthew 9:36 . . .	Compassionate
Remembers failures	Isaiah 43:25; Psalm 103:12; Micah 7:19	Harbors no grudge
Forgets efforts	Hebrews 6:10	Remembers your efforts
Changes	Hebrews 13:8; James 1:17; Isaiah 54:10	Immutable
Is full of sin	1 John 3:5; Hebrews 7:26; Hebrews 4:15	Sinless

God Is Not a Man Illustration, David Stephens *Discovering Who He Is*, (Tulsa: D-Vine Focus, 1989), page 1.

GOD IS TRUSTWORTHY

DAY 1

SCRIPTURE MEMORY
God Is Trustworthy
■ **1 Kings 8:23**
■ **Psalm 89:34**
■ **Psalm 111:7-8**

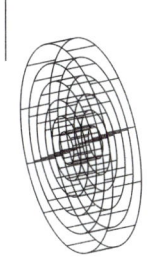

A friend comes to you at the end of her rope with a problem. She has tried everything to come up with a solution, and nothing has worked. She asks for your advice, but it's obvious the solution is beyond your own wisdom and knowledge so you say, "Give it to God; you can trust Him." She asks, "Why should I trust God?"

1. How would you answer this question?

It's one thing to say that God is trustworthy. It's another thing to trust Him completely.

2. Check areas below where you trust God easily. Underline areas where it is not so easy to trust God.

- ❑ Salvation
- ❑ Money
- ❑ Dating life
- ❑ Lifestyle/morality
- ❑ Your future
- ❑ Friendships

- ❑ Health
- ❑ Future marriage partner
- ❑ Trials
- ❑ Your heart's desires
- ❑ Forgiveness
- ❑ Answered prayer

It's easy to make check marks. It's easy to trust God for health when you are healthy. It's easy to make your own plans for the future and decide that God must want that too. But have you really given these things to the Lord?

Commit your way to the Lord, Trust also in Him, and He will do it (Ps. 37:5).

3. According to these passages why is God trustworthy?

Nehemiah 9:6

1 Kings 8:23-24

Psalm 9:7-10

Psalm 31:14-15

Psalm 89:34

Psalm 108:4

Psalm 111:7-8

Jeremiah 32:27

Titus 1:2

4. Are you more likely to trust an acquaintance or someone with whom you share a deep relationship? Why?

Those who know Thy name will put their trust in Thee; For Thou, O Lord, hast not forsaken those who seek Thee (Ps. 9:10).

5. Write your week 2 memory verse ("Fellowship with God").

6. What is the relationship between the quality of fellowship you experience with God and your willingness to trust Him?

Tim Hansel writes, "One day, while my son Zac and I were out in the country, climbing around in some cliffs, I heard a voice from above me yell, 'Hey Dad! Catch me!' I turned around to see Zac joyfully jumping off a rock straight at me. He had jumped and *then* yelled 'Hey Dad!' I became an instant circus act, catching him. We both fell to the ground... I gasped in exasperation: 'Zac! Can you give me *one* good reason why you did that???' "

"He responded with remarkable calmness: 'Sure... *because you're my Dad.*' His whole assurance was based in the fact that his father was trustworthy."[1]

DAY 2

When the ground shakes, we run to what we believe to be solid ground. When trials come into our lives, our concept of God is revealed in deeper ways. Do we see God as capable of bearing our burdens or do we take them to another seemingly reliable source?

Read Psalm 56:1-13.

7. Why was David, the writer of this psalm, tempted with fear? (vv. 1-3)

8. What was his shield against such a temptation? (vv. 3-4)

9. In verses 5-6 how does David specifically answer his own question, "What can mere men do to me?

10. What was his concept of God? (vv. 8-12)

11. How did this concept enable him to get a grip on his situation?

12. What in your life is causing fear or stress?

13. How does this passage encourage you to trust God with this issue?

Hannah Whitall Smith writes, "You can simply refuse to doubt. You can shut the door against every suggestion of doubt that comes, and can by faith declare exactly the opposite... You have no more right to say that you are of such a doubting nature that you cannot help doubting, than to say you are of such a thieving nature that you cannot help thieving. One is as easily controlled as the other. You must give up your doubting just as you would give up your thieving. You must treat the temptation to doubt exactly as a drunkard must treat the temptation to drink; you must take a pledge against it."[3]

DAY 3

As you complete today's lesson, reflect on the trustworthiness of God in your own life—as Savior, as Sustainer, as Provider, as Father, and so much more!

He has made His wonders to be remembered; The Lord is gracious and compassionate (Ps. 111:4).

Read Deuteronomy 8:11-14,18.

14. What may cause us to forget that God is our trust? (vv. 12-14)

15. Verse 11—What results from this forgetfulness?

16. Write your week 5 memory verse ("Idolatry").

The name of the Lord is a strong tower; The righteous runs into it and is safe. A rich man's wealth is his strong city, And like a high wall in his own imagination (Prov. 18:10-11).

17. What can you learn about trust from this passage?

> "The contrast is not between the righteous and the rich in an absolute sense, as there are many people who are both righteous and wealthy. Rather we should see the contrast drawn between the two primary objects of man's trust: God and money. Those who trust in the Lord *are* safe; while those who trust in their wealth only *imagine* they are safe."[2]
> —Jerry Bridges

Alexander MacLaren writes, "If I am to cling with my hand I must first empty my hand. Fancy a man saying, 'I cannot stand unless you hold me up; but I have to hold my bank book, and this thing, and that thing, and the other thing; I cannot put them down, so I have not a hand free to lay hold with, you must do the holding.' Now the prayer, 'Hold Thou me up, and I shall be safe,' is a right one; but not from a man who will not put his possessions out of his hands that he may lay hold of the God who lays hold of him."[4]

Read Psalm 44:1-8.

The psalmist recounts what their fathers had told them about their deliverance from Egypt. He writes of the events, but the emphasis is on the one who performed the deeds.

18. Verse 2—To whom does he give the credit?

19. Verse 3—Who was not the source of their deliverance?

20. How did this knowledge help the psalmist's perspective in his own battles? (vv. 4-8)

"In God we have boasted all day long" (v. 8). Share with a friend or family member about a situation in which you have found the Lord to be trustworthy.

DAY 4

Feelings can become our worst enemies, especially in our relationship with God. We must discipline ourselves so that our emotions don't dictate our level of trust. Think about it. Which should be the object of your faith? Feelings, which are based upon you? Or the character of the Immutable God?

Read Job 23:8-14.

21. How does Job describe his experience with God? (vv. 8-9)

22. Verse 10—What does Job say to indicate that God was with him even though he could not sense His presence?

23. Why did God allow Job to go through these trials? (v. 10)

When we face a trial, our first impulse is to try to get control of the situation so that we can change it. We ask, "What can I do to get out of this mess?

24. What course of action did Job choose? (vv. 11-12)

25. When we are in the midst of oppression or affliction, how do our actions reveal where we have placed our trust?

26. How can you not allow trials to cripple your obedience to the Lord?

27. Verse 12—What does Job say to emphasize the fact that he had gained comfort from the Word of God?

28. Write a verse you have memorized that might help sustain you through a trial.

29. Job could not sense God's presence. He didn't see Him. He wasn't in the middle of an emotional spiritual high. Upon what did he base his choice to trust God? (vv. 10,13,14)

Jerry Bridges writes, "I was a prisoner to my feelings. I mistakenly thought I could not trust God unless I *felt* like trusting Him (which I almost never did in times of adversity). Now I am learning that trusting God is first of all a matter of the will, and is not dependent on my feelings. I choose to trust God and my feelings eventually follow."[6]

30. Upon what must you base your choice in whom you will trust?

Though you have not seen Him, you love Him, and though you do not see Him now, but believe in Him, you greatly rejoice with joy inexpressible and full of glory, obtaining as the outcome of your faith the salvation of your souls (1 Pet. 1:8-9).

DAY 5

Read 1 Samuel 17:1-51.

The Philistines, with their war-like nature, effective political organization, and economic power, were strong rivals of Israel. They were also intensely religious; they carried their idols into battle.

The city of Gath was the nearest of the large Philistine towns to Hebrew territory. It had a reputation for huge men.

31. **What did Goliath look like? (vv. 4-7)**

32. **What was his challenge? (vv. 8-9)**

"He may hide Himself from our sense of His presence, but He never allows our adversities to hide us from Him. He may allow us to pass through the deep waters and the fire, but He will be with us in them."[5]
—Jerry Bridges

33. Verse 11—What was the response of Israel and its leader?

34. Why was David sent to the war camp? (vv. 17-18)

35. Verse 22—Why did David enter the battle line?

36. How does Eliab, David's oldest brother, become the voice of accusation? (vv. 26-28)

37. Verse 32—What does David say he will do?

38. What was the response of King Saul? (vv. 33,38)

39. What was the response of Goliath? (vv. 43-44)

40. What do you notice about David's confidence? (vv. 32,37,45-48)

Max Lucado writes of this event, "The soldiers gasped. Saul sighed. Goliath jeered. David swung. And God made his point. 'Anyone who underestimates what God can do with the ordinary has rocks in his head.' "[7]

David learned a lot on that lonely mountain tending the sheep!

41. How did God prepare David for such an encounter? (vv. 34-35)

42. How does this encourage you to trust in God when you face the "lions" and the "bears" in your life?

[1] *Holy Sweat*, Tim Hansel, 1987, Word Publishing, Nashville, Tennessee. All rights reserved.
[2] *Trusting God*, Jerry Bridges, 1988, 1993. Used by Permission of NavPress/Pinon Press. All rights reserved. For Copies call 1-800-366-7788.
[3] Hannah Whitall Smith, *The God of All Comfort* (New York: Ballantine Books, 1986), 130-131.
[4] Alexander MacLaren, *Expositions of Holy Scripture, Psalms*, 1974, 1977, 36 Baker Book House Company.
[5] *Trusting God*, Bridges, 199.
[6] *Trusting God*, Bridges, 195.
[7] *The Applause of Heaven*, Max Lucado, 1996, Word Publishing, Nashville, Tennessee. All rights reserved.

This week you should know how to share this much of the "God Is Not a Man" Illustration. You should have your seven verses memorized. You should be able to draw this much on a piece of paper.

God Is Not a Man
(Num. 23:19; 1 Sam. 15:29; 1 Cor. 1:25)

Man		God
Willfully hurts. . . . . Lamentations 3:22-23; Psalm 103:8; Matthew 9:36 . . .	Compassionate
Remembers failures . . . . Isaiah 43:25; Psalm 103:12; Micah 7:19	Harbors no grudge
Forgets efforts . . . . Hebrews 6:10.	Remembers your efforts
Changes. . . . . Hebrews 13:8; James 1:17; Isaiah 54:10	Immutable
Is full of sin . . . . 1 John 3:5; Hebrews 7:26; Hebrews 4:15	Sinless
Untrustworthy/unfaithful . . . . . Psalm 111:7-8; Psalm 89:34; 1 Kings 8:23	Trustworthy/faithful

God Is Not a Man Illustration, David Stephens *Discovering Who He Is*, (Tulsa: D-Vine Focus, 1989), page 1.

GOD'S GOODNESS AND JUSTICE

SCRIPTURE MEMORY
Seeking God
■ Psalm 16:2
■ Psalm 42:1
■ Isaiah 26:8

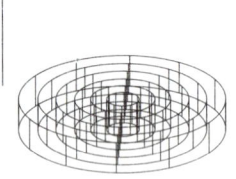

DAY 1

When we look at the goodness of God in the Bible, we find in some Scripture texts that His goodness expresses His kindness. In other places, "It expresses the supreme benevolence, holiness, and excellence of the divine character, the sum of all God's attributes."[1]

One thing we know about God's goodness is that every person, Christian or not, experiences it to some degree. However, as we shall see, not everyone comes to know God in all of His goodness.

The Lord is good to all, And His mercies are over all His works (Ps. 145:9).

As J. I. Packer writes, "The biblical way of putting this distinction would be to say that God is good to all in some ways and to some in all ways."[2]

Read Psalm 65:1-13.

Thou dost visit the earth (v. 9).

1. How does everyone benefit from God's "visit?" (vv. 9-13)

"... for He causes His sun to rise on the evil and the good, and sends rain on the righteous and the unrighteous" (Matt. 5:45).

"Is there any number to His troops? And upon whom does His light not rise?" (Job 25:3).

"In the generations gone by He permitted all the nations to go their own ways; and yet He did not leave Himself without witness, in that He did good and gave you rains from heaven and fruitful seasons, satisfying your hearts with food and gladness" (Acts 14:16-17).

Read Psalm 65:3-4.

2. How is the Lord's goodness experienced?

    Verse 3

    Verse 4

3. Why is this portion of God's goodness not experienced by everyone?

4. How does God use the blessings mentioned in verses 9-13 to whet our spiritual appetites?

This is where we begin to understand how God's goodness also relates to His kindness. Look at Romans 2:4 in the following two translations.

Despisest thou the riches of his goodness and forbearance and longsuffeing; not knowing that the goodness of God leadeth thee to repentance? (Rom. 2:4, KJV).

Do you show contempt for the riches of his kindness, tolerance and patience, not realizing that God's kindness leads you toward repentance? (Rom. 2:4, NIV).

5. What can the blessings in verses 3-4 promise that those in verses 9-13 cannot?

6. Do you think that experiencing the Lord's goodness (vv. 3-4) will enable you to have a greater appreciation for the blessings mentioned in verses 9-13? Explain.

DAY 2

We spend a large portion of our lives accumulating what is good. We desire good relationships, a good education, good food, good luck, good mornings, good nights, good humor, good morals, and on and on. Then at some point we look around and discover that in some ways the term *good* is pretty generic. What one person considers "good" is rejected by another. Yet we know down deep that there *are* definitions in this life.

This fact draws us to the Standard by which all "good" is measured. After being confronted with God Himself, we find that at our best we are really good-for-nothing; and that the things we deem as "good" are not necessarily the best.

C. S. Lewis writes, "The Divine 'goodness' differs from ours, but it is not sheerly different: it differs from ours not as white from black but as a perfect circle from a child's first attempt to draw a wheel. But when the child has learned to draw, it will know the circle it then makes is what it was trying to make from the very beginning."[4]

7. What are some "good" things that you have not yet accumulated but that you would like to possess?

8. Write your week 13 memory verse ("Prayer").

I said to the Lord, "Thou art my Lord; I have no good besides Thee" (Ps. 16:2).

9. If you were to see a prayer request list from each of these psalmists, what do the following verses indicate might be on their lists?

Psalm 42:1-2

Psalm 104:34

Psalm 143:6

10. What is the difference between seeking God for the good He can do or give, and seeking God for God Himself?

11. What can you learn from the deer in Psalm 42:1 and the parched land in Psalm 143:6?

12. Read Habakkuk 3:17-18. What application can you gain from this passage for the times when the Lord seems to withhold good things from you?

The good things from heaven are overwhelming: the power to overcome sin, strength to live above the world, contentment, peace, joy, salvation, forgiveness, eternity, heavenly mansions prepared for us by the Master Carpenter, and so forth. But these things in themselves are not God. Their claim of goodness lies in the fact that God is their Source. The lesson is simply this: seek God and *then* seek good, not the other way around!

"God Himself is the heart's desire of those who delight in Him; and the blessedness of longing fixed on Him is that it ever fulfils itself. They who want God have Him. Your truest joy is in His fellowship and His grace. If, set free from creatural delights, our wills reach out towards God, as a plant growing in darkness to the light—then we shall wish for nothing contrary to Him, and the wishes which run parallel to His purposes, and embrace Himself as their only good, cannot be in vain."[5]

DAY 3

We now shift our attention from the divine perfection of goodness to God's holy justice.

"Justice, when used of God, is a name we give to the way God is, nothing more; and when God acts justly He is not doing so to conform to an independent criterion, but simply acting like Himself in a given situation. ... Everything in the universe is good to the degree it conforms to the nature of God and evil as it fails to do so. God is His own self-existent principle of moral equity, and when He sentences evil men or rewards the righteous, He simply acts like Himself from within, uninfluenced by anything that is not Himself."[7]

"The Bible clearly teaches that God is the Supreme Judge of the universe. ... To function as the Supreme Judge of heaven and earth, He ought to be just. If the Supreme Judge is unjust, we have no hope of justice ever prevailing. We know that earthly judges can be corrupt. They take bribes; they show partiality; at times they act from ignorance. They make mistakes."

"Not so with God. There is no corruption in Him. No one can bribe Him. He refuses to show partiality. He is no respecter of persons. He never acts out of ignorance. He does not make mistakes."[8]

Read Genesis 18:17-33.

13. How does Abraham describe injustice in verses 23 and 25?

14. Verse 20—What had the people in the cities of Sodom and Gomorrah done to bring about such an action from the Lord?

15. How does Abraham appeal to the Lord's justice in this passage?

16. What does God promise to Abraham?

Read Genesis 19:12-17,24-29.

17. What did the two angels urge Lot and his family to do? (vv. 12-17)

18. What did the angels warn Lot and his family not to do when they left the city? (v. 17)

19. Where did Lot go? (v. 23)

20. What happened to Sodom and Gomorrah? (vv. 24-25)

> "God's justice is never divorced from His righteousness. He never condemns the innocent. He never clears the guilty. He never punishes with undo severity. He never fails to reward righteousness. His justice is perfect justice."[6]
> —R. C. Sproul

21. What happened to Lot's wife? (v. 26)

22. How do we see God's justice demonstrated in these events?

23. Does God's justice here seem reasonable or harsh to you? Explain.

24. Do you ever wish that God would demonstrate His justice toward the
    ungodly? Explain.

Read 2 Peter 2:4-9.

25. Who experienced the justice of God?

    Verse 4

    Verse 5

    Verse 6

26. Who experienced the mercy of God?

    Verse 5

    Verse 7

27. Verse 9—How do the righteous experience God's mercy today?

28. Verse 9—How will the unrighteous experience His justice?

DAY 4

The sins of Israel were so numerous that injustice seemed to be the rule of
the land. In today's passage the prophet Isaiah cries out in fading hope that
justice would return and that salvation would come. God gives him a prophetic
picture of the only One who could accomplish this.

Read Isaiah 59:3-20.

29. According to the following verses how had God's people given
    themselves over to sin?

    hands (vv. 3,6)

    fingers (v. 3)

lips (vv. 3-4)

tongue (v. 3)

mind (vv. 4,7)

feet (vv. 7-8)

30. Verse 2—What were the consequences of their sin?

31. Where did this separation leave them?

Verse 9

Verse 10

Verse 11

Verse 12

Verse 14

32. What is the difference between verse 14 and the end of verse 16?

"Redemptive theology teaches that mercy does not become effective toward a man until justice has done its work. The just penalty for sin was exacted when Christ our Substitute died for us on the cross."[10]

33. Write your week 10 memory verse ("God Harbors No Grudge").

34. Verse 17—How does God's attire characterize His goodness and justice?

35. How is His justice characterized in verse 18?

36. How is His goodness characterized in verse 20?

37. Verse 19—What is the ultimate result of His goodness and justice?

DAY 5

Though the wicked may prosper, there is a limit to their favor. Their prosperity cannot cross over into eternity. And as today's passage will teach us, it is impossible for the wicked to even begin to grasp what is most valuable. As God's children, we have been given the mind of Christ (1 Cor. 2:16). May this truth convince our understanding that *He* is the desire of our souls.

Read Isaiah 26:7-10.

38. What do the righteous determine to be the ultimate good? (vv. 8-9)

39. Verse 9—What do the Lord's judgments upon the earth teach its inhabitants?

40. Verse 10—And yet who has not grasped this lesson?

The message of verse 10 seems to be that though outwardly the wicked may prosper to a certain extent, they cannot enjoy the best that life has to offer.

41. What does Isaiah determine to be the real "stuff of life"?

42. Verse 7—What promise can you claim as you embrace God as your ultimate good?

[1]Taken from *The New Unger's Bible Dictionary* by Merrill F. Unger, Moody Press, © 1957, 1961, 1966. Used by permission.

[2]J. I. Packer, *Knowing God* (Downers Grove, Illinois: InterVarsity Press, 1973), 162.

[3]Scripture quotations marked (NIV) are from the Holy Bible, *New International Version.* Copyright © 1973, 1978, 1984 by International Bible Society.

[4]C. S. Lewis, *The Problem of Pain* (New York: Macmillan Publishing Company 1962, 1976), 39.

[5]Alexander MacLaren, *Expositions of Holy Scripture, Psalms,* 1974, 1977, Baker Book House.

[6]From *The Holiness of God* by R. C. Sproul, © 1985. Used by permission of Tyndale House Publishers, Inc. All rights reserved.

[7]A. W. Tozer, *The Knowledge of the Holy* (San Francisco: Harper & Row Publishers, 1961), 93-94.

[8]*The Holiness of God,* Sproul, 143.

[9]Rebecca Manley Pippert, *Hope Has Its Reasons* (San Francisco: Harper & Row, Publishers, 1989), 94.

[10]Tozer, *The Knowledge of the Holy,* 94-95.

WEEK 19
THE LOVE OF GOD

DAY 1

SCRIPTURE MEMORY
The Love of God
■ Romans 5:8
■ Romans 8:38-39
■ 1 John 4:10

1. **What do we do to the meaning of the word** *love* **when we use it to express so many different sentiments? ("I** *love* **rocky road ice cream." "I** *love* **snow-capped mountains." "I** *love* **my mom." "I** *love* **God.")**

As we study God's love we must understand that though the combination of these four letters are very familiar to us, God's love is a love which is set apart from anything we know as love–just as the Holy God Himself is set apart from anything and everything that we are acquainted with on this earth.

Love is translated in the Greek language as *Phileo* which is brotherly love and *Eros* which is the sexual love between man and woman. But the Greek word that expresses God's love for us is something different entirely.

J. I. Packer writes, "The New Testament writers had to introduce what was virtually a new Greek word *agape* to express the love of God as they knew it."[1]

Read 1 John 4:7-12.

Verse 8 says that "God is love." God is *agape*. What is agape love?

2. **Match each response on the right to the correct description on the left. References are from 1 John 4.**

___ Love's originator (v. 7)   A. Human beings
___ Love's messenger (v. 9)   B. God
___ Love's object (v. 10)   C. Jesus

3. **Why do you think John emphasizes in verse 10 that love is not realized in our love for God but in His love for us?**

4. **First John 4:12 says, "No one has beheld God at any time." How can we make God "visible" to the world? (See vv. 7,11-12.)**

5. **If we make God visible to the world what will He "look" like? (For a description of agape love read 1 Cor. 13:4-8.)**

6. **How is love the evidence that Christ lives in your heart? (vv. 7-8)**

We have examined how God's character is the extreme opposite of man's character. His thoughts are not our thoughts. His natural response is not our natural response. And when it comes to His love—well, again, we find something different from ourselves entirely.

7. Answer yes or no to the following questions:

❏ yes ❏ no Have you ever made a promise to God that you failed to keep?

❏ yes ❏ no Do you think God loves you less because you did not keep it?

❏ yes ❏ no Have you ever been obedient to follow through with something God told you to do?

❏ yes ❏ no Do you think God loves you more because you did it?

Read Romans 5:5-8.

8. Verse 7—How far will human-based love go?

9. How does God's love extend beyond human love? (vv. 6, 8)

10. God's love for us was . . . (check one or more)

❏ an exhilarated feeling
❏ spoken in words
❏ demonstrated by action

11. God's love was based upon . . . (check one or more)

❏ our past faithfulness
❏ the potential of what we might become
❏ God Himself

His own love toward us . . . (v. 5:8a).

Man's Love	God's Love
• Given only as it is received.	• Given whether returned or not.
• Based upon man's nature.	• Based upon God's nature. Active.
• Emotional.	
• Given until weaknesses are exposed.	• Knows all weaknesses already and loves in spite of them.
• Manipulates for selfish gain.	• Creates the freedom to not choose Him.
• Can change overnight.	• Incapable of change or separation.

12. What would result if we perceived God's love to "look" like man's?

G. Campbell Morgan writes, "Creation was an act of love, and all law is an expression of love. Love for ever suffers when the loved one suffers. I sometimes think that the difference between God's love and my love at its highest lies just there. I love; and if the one I love is untrue to me, I suffer. Why? Because I have lost that love. God does not suffer in that way. He suffers because the one who ceases to love Him is suffering. There is an element of self in our love. There is none in God's."[2]

13. Review Romans 5:6-8 and write what these verses reveal about unconditional love.

14. Write your week 3 memory verse ("The Holy Spirit").

15. Look at Romans 5:5. What does the Holy Spirit do in relation to us and God's love?

16. What implications does this truth have for the way you can now love others?

DAY 3

What we continue to discover about *Agape* love is that it is not based upon whether a person is deserving of it, nor is it based upon whether a person *doesn't* deserve it. What we discover about God's love for His children is that it is based upon *Who He* is.

17. Check any of the following that you think seem to distance you as a Christian from God's love.

- ❑ death
- ❑ premarital sex
- ❑ denying Christ
- ❑ Satan
- ❑ you
- ❑ disobedience
- ❑ parents
- ❑ rebellion

Read Romans 8:31-39.

Verses 31-34 help us to better understand the magnitude of God's love.

18. Verse 33—"Who will bring a charge against God's elect?" When God had a right to bring a charge against us, what did He do instead?

19. Verse 34—"Who is the one who condemns?" When Jesus had the right to condemn us what did He do instead?

If God is for us . . . (v. 31).

20. Considering what you have written and re-examining verse 32, what is the greatest evidence "that God is for us"?

Delivered Him up for us all, how will He not also with Him freely give us all things? (v. 32).

The message of verse 32 is this: God led His Son to the slaughter with our sins on His back. Afterward Jesus rose from the dead to make us joint-heirs of His estate.

21. Describe the inheritance He has given to us in regard to the following:

blessings (v. 32)

position (v. 34)

intervention (v. 34)

authority (v. 37)

22. Write your week 15 memory verse ("God Is Immutable").

23. Read verses 38-39. What does this passage say in relation to the things that seem to distance you as a Christian from God's love?

24. Meditate on verses 38-39. What thoughts come to mind ?

"Many waters cannot quench love, Nor will rivers overflow it" (Song of Sol. 8:7).

DAY 4

Today's passage draws us near to the heart of God as we see His unrelenting love for His rebellious and ungrateful chosen nation.

Read Hosea 11:1-11.

25. How was God's love affirmed to Israel?

Verse 1

Verse 3

Verse 4

26. How did Israel respond to God's love?

Verse 2

Verse 5

Verse 7

27. Admah and Zeboim were two cities of the valley of Siddim which were destroyed by fire from heaven along with Sodom and Gomorrah. What are the questions that God asks in verse 8?

28. What does God declare in the first part of verse 9 in answer to His questions?

29. Which attribute(s) of God do you think would cause Him to make such declarations?

30. Which attribute is mentioned in verse 9?

"When God, in spite of sin, says, 'How can I give you up? My heart is stirred, My compassions are stirred, but I am holy; how can I give you up?' and yet says, 'I will not give you up, I will not, I will not,' we are in the presence of some possibility wholly of God"[4]

So My people are bent on turning from Me (v. 7).

31. Even after all that God had done for Israel, His people had an aversion to follow Him. As God's people, how are we similar or different in following Him today?

In verse 8 God says, "all my compassions are kindled." Think of something that causes your compassions to be kindled. Maybe it is an orphaned puppy shivering in the snow, or the poverty of a hungry third-world child. Perhaps it is a friend who has experienced the tragic loss of someone close. Your heart goes out to those who hurt.

Yet, look again at this verse. God's compassions are not kindled because of His heart's going out to Israel. Israel had done nothing to deserve His love. Instead look at what the verse says, "My heart is turned over within Me."

32. When God could find no reason to be merciful toward Israel, His compassions were kindled because of the love within Him. What does this say about the way God loves us today?

33. How will God's people respond to such a love? (vv. 10-11)

Do you think lightly of the riches of His kindness and forbearance and patience, not knowing that the kindness of God leads you to repentance? (Rom. 2:4).

34. In discovering the vastness of God's love, how does it affect the way you want to live your life?

DAY 5

35. Write your week 4 memory verse ("Abiding in Christ").

Read John 15:1-11.

As a branch of the Vine, we are, in essence, an extension of Christ's life. So then, our love for others is, in essence, an extension of Christ's love in us. What this means is that it is Christ Himself who gives us the ability to love. As we consider today's passage, we will discover that if we are to demonstrate love to others, there is really no other way but to demonstrate Christ's love.

Read 1 John 4:16-21.

36. Verse 16—How can you know that you are abiding in Christ?

37. What is the difference between fear and confidence? (vv. 17-18)

38. Look at the following translations of the last part of verse 17.

We realize that our life in this world is actually his life lived in us (1 John 4:17, Phillips).[5]

As he is, so are we in this world (1 John 4:17, KJV).

because in this world we are like Him (1 John 4:17, NIV).[6]

39. Why is this truth the basis of our confidence?

J. B. Phillips translates 1 John 4:8 like this, "Love contains no fear–indeed fully-developed love expels every particle of fear, for fear always contains some of the torture of feeling guilty. The man who lives in fear has not yet had his love perfected."[7]

Sometimes we wear a guilt complex as if it were a "crown of thorns," a seemingly self-defacing, but prized spiritual trophy. We think that the more wretched and worthless we esteem ourselves, the more fortunate heaven is to have us in its grasp.

40. Yet, what does this presumption really reveal according to verse 18?

Now, little children, abide in Him, so that when He appears, we may have confidence and not shrink away from Him in shame at His coming. If you know that He is righteous, you know that everyone also who practices righteousness is born of Him (1 John 2:28-29).

A life that is perfected in love–a life that is abiding in Christ–will be a life which is also characterized by righteousness.

41. Which of the following do you think would bring greater confidence to live in obedience to all that God commands?

❑ The person who is burdened with guilt.
❑ The person who accepts her position in Christ even in the middle of spiritual failures.

42. Why do we tend to place our confidence in our love for God rather than His love for us?

43. Verse 19—Why is it important to understand who initiates the love relationship we have with God?

44. Think of the person you like least. Your love for that person, is the same as your love for God. Do you agree or disagree? Explain.

> "Do not waste time bothering whether you 'love' your neighbor; act as if you did. As soon as we do this we find one of the great secrets. When you are behaving as if you loved someone, you will presently come to love him. If you injure someone you dislike, you will find yourself disliking him more. If you do him a good turn, you will find yourself disliking him less."[8]
> —C. S. Lewis

There will always be people in your life who are hard to love. But just as God's love for us is based upon who He is and not what we are, our love for others must be based upon who God is and the example we have in His Word.

45. Think seriously for a moment. How can we apply this truth to those people who are difficult to love?

46. Complete the following sentence: If I allow myself to love someone, he/she might ... (think of several options.)

"There is no safe investment. To love at all is to be vulnerable. Love anything, and your heart will certainly be wrung and possibly be broken. If you want to make sure of keeping it intact, you must give your heart to no one, not even to an animal. Wrap it carefully round with hobbies and little luxuries; avoid all entanglements; lock it up safe in the casket or coffin of your selfishness. But in that casket—safe, dark, motionless, airless—it will change. It will not be broken; it will become unbreakable, impenetrable, irredeemable. The alternative to tragedy, or at least to the risk of tragedy, is damnation. The only place outside Heaven where you can be perfectly safe from all the dangers and perturbations of love is Hell."[9]

Now may our Lord Jesus Christ Himself and God our Father, who has loved us and given us eternal comfort and good hope by grace, comfort and strengthen your hearts in every good work and word (2 Thess. 2:16-17).

[1] J. I. Packer, *Knowing God* (Downers Grove, Illinois: InterVarsity Press, 1973), 112.
[2] G. Campbell Morgan, *Hosea: The Heart and Holiness of God* (London: Marshall Morgan & Scott LTD., 1960), 19
[3] Ibid.
[4] Ibid.
[5] Reprinted with permission of Macmillan Publishing Co., Inc. from J. B. Phillips: *The New Testament in Modern English*, Revised Edition. © J. B. Phillips 1958, 1960, 1972.
[6] Scripture quotations marked (NIV) are from the Holy Bible, *New International Version*. Copyright © 1973, 1978, 1984 by International Bible Society.
[7] Phillips, *The Testament in Modern English*.
[8] *Mere Christianity* by C. S. Lewis copyright © C. S. Lewis Pte. Ltd. 1942, 1943, 1944, 1952. Extract reprinted by permission.
[9] C. S. Lewis, *The Four Loves* (New York: Inspirational Press, 1994), 278-279.

This week you should know how to share this much of the "God Is Not a Man" Illustration. You should have your eight verses memorized. You should be able to draw this much on a piece of paper.

God Is Not a Man
(Num. 23:19; 1 Sam. 15:29; 1 Cor. 1:25)

Man		**God**
Willfully hurts	Lamentations 3:22-23; Psalm 103:8; Matthew 9:36 . . .	Compassionate
Remembers failures	Isaiah 43:25; Psalm 103:12; Micah 7:19	Harbors no grudge
Forgets efforts	Hebrews 6:10	Remembers your efforts
Changes	Hebrews 13:8; James 1:17; Isaiah 54:10	Immutable
Is full of sin	1 John 3:5; Hebrews 7:26; Hebrews 4:15	Sinless
Untrustworthy/unfaithful	Psalm 111:7-8; Psalm 89:34; 1 Kings 8:23	Trustworthy/faithful
Loves conditionally	Romans 5:8; 1 John 4:10; Romans 8:38-39	Loves unconditionally

God Is Not a Man Illustration, David Stephens *Discovering Who He Is,* (Tulsa: D-Vine Focus, 1989), 1.

METHODS OF BIBLE STUDY (1 THESSALONIANS)

SCRIPTURE MEMORY
God Is Infallible
■ Deuteronomy 31:8

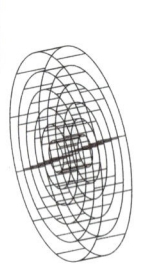

This week you will study the Book of 1 Thessalonians using one or more of the four methods of Bible study introduced in week 8: Ready, Aim, Fire Method; The P's and Q's Method; The Triple S Method; The John 15:5 Method. You may want to refer to week 8 for an example of each method.

Ready, Aim, Fire Method

Ready—*Bring the principles into focus.* Write points or facts the passage reveals.

Aim—*Finding the target.* What verse stands out to you most?

Fire—*What does my "target verse" challenge me to do?* How can I put into practice what this verse is saying? What specific commitment do I need to make to live out the truth of this verse?

The P's and Q's Method

P's–*Principles.* Write down the principles the passage teaches.

Q's–*Questions.* Answer the following questions in regard to the principles you discovered in the passage.

What sin do I need to confess?

What example do I need to model?

What command do I need to obey?

Application. Upon answering the questions, what action do I need to take?

The Triple S Method

Standard—State the principle or ideal expressed from one particular verse.

Struggles—How am I not measuring up to this (ideal or principle) in my life?

Strategy—My course of action to change this. How can I apply the Scripture to my problem?

The John 15:5 Method

1. "I am the Vine"—What does this passage reveal about God or Jesus Christ?
2. "You are the branches"—What does this passage reveal about me?
3. "He who abides in Me and I in Him bears much fruit"–What verse from this passage is the Holy Spirit using to prune me so that His fruit can be produced in my life?
4. "For apart from Me you can do nothing"—Pray the following:

Lord, I realize that the first step in applying this truth in my life is to admit that without You I cannot do it. So, I give this to You right now and thank You that no matter what happens, You have taken it. Let me not listen to the voice of the deceiver, who wants me to feel defeated. Let me not trust in my own strength and try to accomplish this in my flesh. But may I place my hope and my trust in You that through Jesus You can accomplish this in me. Amen.

It is important to be specific in your applications. Below are examples of applications for Galatians 6:2, "Bear one another's burdens and thus fulfill the law of Christ."

Okay: "I will help others more."

Good: "I will be sensitive to someone in need and make myself available to them."

Better: "My mom has had a heavy workload lately so I will bear her burden by helping more around the house."

Best: "God is specifically leading me through this verse to help my mom more around the house since she has had a lot of stress at work. I will do the dishes all week without being asked (whether my brother does his share or not). I will take my brother to soccer practice."

Prove yourselves doers of the word, and not merely hearers who delude themselves (Jas. 1:22).

DAY 1

Ready, Aim, Fire Method
1 Thessalonians 1

Ready—*Bring the principles into focus.*

Aim—*Finding the target.*

Fire—*What does my "target verse" challenge me to do?*

The P's and Q's Method
1 Thessalonians 2

P's–_Principles_

Q's–_Questions_

What sin do I need to confess?

What example do I need to model?

What command do I need to obey?

Application

The Triple S Method
1 Thessalonians 3

Standard

Struggles

Strategy

The John 15:5 Method
1 Thessalonians 4

1. "I am the Vine"—What is this saying about God or Jesus Christ?

2. "You are the branches"—What does this passage reveal about me?

3. "He who abides in Me and I in Him bears much fruit"—What verse from this passage is the Holy Spirit using to prune me so that His fruit can be produced in my life?

4. "For apart from Me you can do nothing"—Pray the following.

Lord, I realize that the first step in applying this truth in my life is to admit that without You I cannot do it. So, I give this to You right now and thank You that no matter what happens, You have taken it. Let me not listen to the voice of the deceiver, who wants me to feel defeated. Let me not trust my own strength and try to accomplish this in my flesh. But may I place my hope and my trust in You that through Jesus You can accomplish all things in me. Amen.

DAY 5

Have fun doing your Bible study today. Check one of the following four Bible study methods and apply it to the Scripture passage provided.

❏ **Ready, Aim, Fire Method**
❏ **The P's and Q's Method**
❏ **The Triple S Method**
❏ **The John 15:5 Method**

1 Thessalonians 5

This week you should know how to share this much of the "God Is Not a Man" Illustration. You should have your nine verses memorized. You should be able to draw this much on a piece of paper.

God Is Not a Man
(Num. 23:19; 1 Sam. 15:29; 1 Cor. 1:25)

Man		God
Willfully hurts	Lamentations 3:22-23; Psalm 103:8; Matthew 9:36 . . .	Compassionate
Remembers failures	Isaiah 43:25; Psalm 103:12; Micah 7:19	Harbors no grudge
Forgets efforts	Hebrews 6:10	Remembers your efforts
Changes	Hebrews 13:8; James 1:17; Isaiah 54:10	Immutable
Is full of sin	1 John 3:5; Hebrews 7:26; Hebrews 4:15	Sinless
Untrustworthy/unfaithful	Psalm 111:7-8; Psalm 89:34; 1 Kings 8:23	Trustworthy/faithful
Loves conditionally	Romans 5:8; 1 John 4:10; Romans 8:38-39	Loves unconditionally
Fallible/undependable	Deuteronomy 31:8	Infallible/dependable

God Is Not a Man Illustration, David Stephens *Discovering Who He Is,* (Tulsa: D-Vine Focus, 1989), 1.

WEEK 21
FAITH

DAY 1

SCRIPTURE MEMORY
Faith
■ Romans 4:20-21
■ Hebrews 11:1
■ Hebrews 11:6

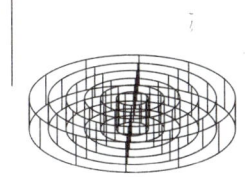

Read Hebrews 11:1-6.

This wonderful New Testament passage begins with a definition of what faith is. Look at the following translations of verse 1.

Faith means that we have full confidence in the things we hope for, it means being certain of things we cannot see (Heb. 11:1, Phillips). [1]

Faith is being sure of what we hope for and certain of what we do not see (Heb. 11:1, NIV). [2]

1. Why is faith necessary if we are to have a relationship with God?

2. Consider the familiar phrase, "Seeing is believing." Does this statement support or contradict the biblical faith defined in verse 1? Explain.

Faith treats the invisible as though it were visible.

3. Verse 3—What does faith allow your mind to accept as fact?

4. Faith allows us to visualize an invisible God. How does faith also allow God to visualize us? (v. 2)

5. Check which of the following correctly completes the sentence: By faith ... (v. 4)

❑ Abel was acceptable to God because his sacrifices were righteous.
❑ Abel's sacrifices were acceptable to God because he was acceptable to God.

Faith comes first, and then acceptance.

6. Check which of the following correctly completes the sentence: By faith ... (v. 5)

❑ Enoch pleased God after he was taken up.
❑ Enoch was taken up because he was pleasing to God.

Faith comes first, then the reward.

7. Verse 6—What does God want you to believe about Him?

8. What do you think is the significance of the word *impossible* in this verse?

DAY 2

Read Luke 17:11-19.

In this passage we see three aspects of faith.

9. Verse 12—What evidence is there from this verse that the lepers wanted Jesus to heal them?

10. Verse 13—What evidence is there from this verse that the lepers believed that Jesus could heal them?

A priest had to certify that a leper was clean (Lev. 14); that is why Jesus in verse 14 tells the lepers to show themselves to the priest.

11. How do the lepers demonstrate the kind of faith that treats the invisible as though it were visible?

12. When were the lepers cleansed? (check one)

❑ When they wanted Jesus to heal them.
❑ When they believed that Jesus could heal them.
❑ When they acted upon His Word.

It would be easy to get the idea that faith simply believes that God can do anything. But this is only part of it. Satan and his demons have this kind of faith. James 2:19 says, "You believe that God is one. You do well; the demons also believe and shudder."

This kind of faith is not the faith that pleases God. Satan's faith does not please God. The faith that pleases God acts upon His Word.

13. How did the lepers act upon the Word of God? (v. 14)

14. What is the difference between the healing in verse 14 and the healing in verse 19?

15. Verse 15—What should be the ultimate result of the blessings received through faith? (check one)

    ❑ that we are satisfied
    ❑ that God is glorified

16. Consider the one leper who "turned back." What do you think might be observed in his lifestyle in the days, weeks, and even years after his healing? Why?

17. Consider the other nine. What do you think might be observed in their lifestyles in the days, weeks and even years after their healings? Why?

18. Who do you relate to the most? Why?

    ❑ the one leper
    ❑ the nine lepers

DAY 3

By faith Abraham, when he was called, obeyed by going out to a place which he was to receive for an inheritance; and he went out, not knowing where he was going. By faith he lived as an alien in the land of promise, as in a foreign land, dwelling in tents with Isaac and Jacob, fellow heirs of the same promise; for he was looking for the city which has foundations, whose architect and builder is God (Heb. 11:8-10).

As the above Scripture remembers the faith of Abraham, let's examine what we can learn from God's Word as we walk by faith today.

Read Romans 4:13-25; 5:1-2.

In hope against hope he believed (Rom. 4:18).

19. In whom did Abraham place his hope? What was the object of his faith? (v. 17)

20. We may say, "If I just had more *faith* I know that God would answer my prayers." What happens when *faith* becomes the object of our faith?

21. Verse 19—What facts did Abraham's faith "stare in the face"?

"Every time you venture out in the life of faith, you will find something in your common-sense circumstances that flatly contradicts your faith ... Can you trust Jesus Christ where your common-sense cannot trust Him? Can you venture heroically on Jesus Christ's statements when the facts of your common-sense life shout—'It's a lie?' ... Let me say I believe God will supply all my need, and then let me run dry, with no outlook, and see whether I will go through the trial of faith, or whether I will sink back to something lower."[3]

22. Abraham "did not waver in unbelief" (v. 20). Why might the facts of verse 19 tempt him to waver in unbelief?

23. Yet, where did Abraham place his confidence? (vv. 20-21)

24. How does Abraham's example encourage you to walk by faith?

Stewart Briscoe tells of a time when he came home and told his wife the happy news that they were going on a two-week vacation. Her response was not the enthusiasm he expected. Since they had a very limited income (he was a preacher) she reacted as though it were a cruel joke. She presumed he either ...
  (1) didn't mean it.
  (2) couldn't afford it.
  (3) was too big of a tight wad.

But then he told her that "Ed Smith" had already taken care of the financial end of it and had secured the time off for them.

When she heard the name, "Ed Smith," her attitude completely changed because she knew that he ...
  (1) was not a person who would say something he didn't mean.
  (2) could easily afford it.
  (3) was naturally generous.

What name would bring such confidence to you? Think of a wealthy person whom you know. If he called you tomorrow and said, "Today I'm depositing enough money in your bank account to cover your needs for life," how would you react?

God says to you that He "shall supply all your needs according to His riches in glory in Christ Jesus" (Phil. 4:19). Do you have more confidence in God or in the wealthy man to secure your future?

25. What does this illustration reveal to you about your concept of God?

26. What are the results of your faith in God as demonstrated in the example of Abraham? (v. 22)

The object of Jewish faith was the law. The Jews placed their confidence in their deeds–in keeping the law. But if a person is made right by the law, then it places God under obligation and closes the door to grace through faith.

It's significant to understand here that faith pre-dates the law.

What I am saying is this: the Law, which came four hundred and thirty years later, does not invalidate a covenant previously ratified by God (Gal. 3:17).

So God made a covenant with Abraham based on faith before he gave the law to Moses. The Jews regarded whatever came first historically as superior to what followed, so Paul places specific emphasis here.

If the inheritance is based on law, it is no longer based on a promise; but God has granted it to Abraham by means of a promise" (Gal. 3:18).

The purpose of the law was to:
(1) Specify transgressions or sins.
(2) Prepare the people for Christ's coming.

Therefore, the Law has become our tutor to lead us to Christ, that we may be justified by faith (Gal. 3:24).

The word *tutor* here means "child conductor." It's a nanny. It's the picture of someone who takes the child to school rather than teaching her at school. Christ is the school; the law brings us to Him.

27. With our own confidence removed from our good deeds, where do we shift our faith? (vv. 24-25)

28. What does this faith enable us to claim? (Rom. 5:1-2)

By grace you have been saved through faith; and that not of yourselves, it is the gift of God; not as a result of works, that no one should boast (Eph. 2:8-9).

DAY 4

"Many busy themselves trying to find more faith, when they have had all they needed right along. I would like you to think of faith a little differently, as an organ like an ear or an eye ... Faith is an organ of the Spirit allowing us to receive whatever God is doing. We can readily see why if we have faith as a mustard seed we can move a mountain; the eye of an ant and the eye of a camel both receive light. Faith itself, not quantity of faith, is the issue."[4]
—Michael Wells

29. Briefly describe how you place your faith in the following:

Your alarm clock

Your shower faucet

A chair

The person at the intersection who faces a red traffic light as you pass through the green light

30. How much effort does it take for you to trust the above?

31. Does faith in God ever seem like something that comes through much effort? Explain.

32. Write your week 7 memory verse ("The Bible, God's Word").

Read Romans 10:13-17.

33. Verse 17—Faith is not generated. It comes through an outside source. What is the outside source?

34. Verse 16—Yet, what does this verse say to indicate that faith does not always come to those who receive this outside source?

Simply acquiring knowledge of Scripture is not enough. Although a person may know the Bible, he can still be without faith.

35. Answer yes or no to the following.

❏ yes ❏ no Have you ever heard a sermon preached and got nothing out of it?

❏ yes ❏ no Have you ever heard a sermon preached (by the same preacher) and received a lot from it?

❏ yes ❏ no Have you ever read a verse of Scripture that seemed to say nothing to you?

❏ yes ❏ no Have you ever read a verse of Scripture (the same one, maybe) and have it leap off the page with just what you needed?

It is not the printed Word itself that brings faith. It is not the preacher speaking the Word that brings faith. It is when Jesus through the Holy Spirit takes that Word or that sermon and speaks it to your heart that brings faith. "Hearing by the Word of Christ" (v. 17). This is when faith comes.

"It is the Spirit who gives life; the flesh profits nothing; the words that I have spoken to you are spirit and are life" (John 6:63).

36. What do you know about Jesus that makes Him worthy of your faith? (Think about some of His attributes which we have reviewed throughout this study.)

37. Look again at some of the things in which you place your faith. Answer yes or no in regard to each.

Your alarm clock
❏ yes ❏ no Is it immutable?
❏ yes ❏ no Is it holy?
❏ yes ❏ no Is it always trustworthy?
❏ yes ❏ no Does it love you?

Your shower faucet
❏ yes ❏ no Is it immutable?
❏ yes ❏ no Is it holy?
❏ yes ❏ no Is it always trustworthy?
❏ yes ❏ no Does it love you?

A chair
❏ yes ❏ no Is it immutable?
❏ yes ❏ no Is it holy?
❏ yes ❏ no Is it always trustworthy?
❏ yes ❏ no Does it love you?

The person at the intersection who faces a red traffic light as you pass through the green light.
❏ yes ❏ no Is he or she immutable?
❏ yes ❏ no Is he or she holy?
❏ yes ❏ no Is he or she always trustworthy?
❏ yes ❏ no Does he or she love you?

38. Why do we tend to place more faith in things than we do in God?

39. According to the following verses what is involved in preparing someone to hear the Word of God?

Verse 14

Verse 15

40. Verse 13—What results from this process?

"Nothing honors God like praising Him for what He promised before the promise is fulfilled. That is the ultimate expression of faith."[3]
—Charles Stanley

DAY 5

Read Mark 11:12-14,20-26.

41. Verse 12—What drew Jesus to the fig tree?

"Seeing at a distance a fig tree in leaf" (v. 13). What's interesting about a fig tree is that it yields its fruit before its leaves, so that if you see leaves you can expect fruit.

"His disciples were listening" (v. 14). So the lesson for the disciples is that if you claim to know Jesus (the "leaves") then your life ought to bring forth fruit (the figs).

42. What does this passage teach us that Jesus "hungers" for in our lives?

Sometimes we keep Christ at a distance. We live life on our own terms. We claim His name for salvation; but we become apathetic in our commitment to Him. We literally try to keep His control–His life-out of us, as we wither. Then we come upon something that is out of our control, maybe a trial that overwhelms us. We try to work up enough faith to get into right standing with Him again. But 2 Corinthians 5:7 says, "we walk by faith, not by sight."

Faith is not something for the "isolation booth." You can't focus your faith toward one desire of your heart without first surrendering all of your heart. You can't leave your faith in the "isolation booth" of your heart's desire and walk through the other areas of your life on your terms. Every step, every decision, every goal is part of the faith walk.

Whatever is not from faith is sin (Rom. 14:23b).

It's important to understand this truth as we look at faith in regard to prayer.

43. Write your week 13 memory verse ("Prayer").

44. Verse 22—When does faith open the door for such supernatural power as described in verse 23?

This is the confidence which we have before Him, that, if we ask anything according to His will, He hears us. And if we know that He hears us in whatever we ask, we know that we have the requests which we have asked from Him (1 John 5:14-15).

45. Verse 24—How is prayer an expression of confidence and faith in God?

46. What hinders our faith? (vv. 25-26)

47. After completing this study, what has God revealed to you that you need to commit to Him in faith?

Give this to Him right now.

Thank God for taking it. And when the accuser tempts you with doubt through feelings and failures, instead of giving it to the Lord again, *thank Him* that He has already taken it—that you have already given it to Him.

---

[1]Reprinted with permission of Macmillan Publishing Co., Inc. from J. B. Phillips: *The New Testament in Modern English*, Revised Edition. © J. B. Phillips 1958, 1960, 1972.

[2]Scripture quotations marked (NIV) are from the Holy Bible, *New International Version*. Copyright © 1973, 1978, 1984 by International Bible Society.

[3]Oswald Chambers, *My Utmost for His Highest* (Westwood, New Jersey: Barbour and Company, Inc., 1935, 1963), 177.

[4]Michael Wells, *Sidetracked in the Wilderness* (Tarrytown, New York: Fleming H. Revell Company, 1991), 67.

[5]Charles Stanley, *The Wonderful Spirit Filled Life* (Nashville: Thomas Nelson, 1992), 150.

WEEK 22
THE FELLOWSHIP OF HIS SUFFERINGS

SCRIPTURE MEMORY
Suffering for Christ
■ Acts 5:40-41
■ 2 Corinthians 1:5
■ 1 Peter 4:1

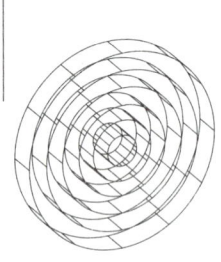

DAY 1

Read Matthew 26:59-68; Matthew 27:1-2,11-50.

1. What did the chief priests and council want to happen? (Matt. 26:59; 27:1)

2. What did they do? (Matt. 26:59-61)

3. How did Jesus suffer according to the following verses?

    Matthew 26:67

    Matthew 27:26

    Matthew 27:28

    Matthew 27:30

4. How did He suffer according to the following verses?

    Matthew 26:68

    Matthew 27:31

    Matthew 27:37-44

5. How did He suffer according to Matthew 27:46?

6. According to the following verses, what was Jesus' response to these sufferings?

    Matthew 26:63

    Matthew 27:12

    Matthew 27:14

7. How does this compare to His response in Matthew 27:46?

He was despised and forsaken of men, A man of sorrows, and acquainted with grief; And like one from whom men hide their face, He was despised, and we did not esteem Him. ... But He was pierced through for our transgressions, He was crushed for our iniquities; The chastening for our well-being fell upon Him, And by His scourging we are healed (Isa. 53:3,5).

8. Describe your thoughts as you think about the sufferings that Jesus endured.

"Surely the disciples stood at Calvary wondering why such a thing was allowed to take place. Humanly speaking, it made no sense at all. But in a few days all the pieces fit together. Often-times we stand like the disciples at Calvary. We watch our hopes and dreams shatter before our eyes. We see our loved ones suffer. We see family members die. And like the disciples, we wonder why."

"We must remember that Christ's death, burial, and resurrection serve as the context of all our suffering. God, through those events, took the greatest tragedy in the history of the world and used it to accomplish His greatest triumph—the salvation of man. If the murder of the perfect Son of God can be explained, how much more can we trust that God is accomplishing His purposes through the adversity we face every day?"[1]

DAY 2

To identify with Christ is to put yourself at risk of suffering at least to some degree. People's negative opinions and rejections probably top the list of pain experienced in present-day America. But in countries around the globe, sharing in Christ's sufferings may mean torture and prison sentences.

If you lived during the first century A.D. and identified yourself with Christ, you risked the chance of dying by some of the most cruel deaths known to man. Consider the deaths of the 11 disciples. (The 12th was Judas.)

Andrew—martyred. Crucified on an X-shaped cross.
Bartholomew—martyred. Flayed alive with knives.
James, son of Zebedee—martyred. Beheaded by Herod in A.D. 44.
James, brother of Jude—martyred. Sawed in pieces.
John, son of Zebedee. Died a natural death.
Jude—martyred. Pierced with arrows.
Matthew—martyred. No one knows or says how.
Peter—martyred. Crucified upside down.
Philip—martyred. Death by hanging.
Simon the Zealot—martyred. Crucified.
Thomas—martyred. Death by spear.

Notice that every disciple except for John died a martyr's death. This means they died for their belief and stand for Christ.

Read Luke 21:12-19.

In this passage, Jesus prophesies to the disciples and others in the synagogues what would happen to them for their belief in Him.

9. What do the following verses reveal about suffering for Christ?

Verse 12

Verse 16

Verse 17

10. What are some ways Christians today might respond to this kind of persecution?

11. When does persecution become a platform? (v. 13)

12. What is promised in the middle of such persecution? (v. 15)

13. What is the reward for standing firm under persecution? (vv. 18-19)

Up until his martyr's death by beheading in Rome, Paul knew what it meant to suffer for the sake of Christ. He wrote about it to his friends in Corinth.

Read 2 Corinthians 11:23-29.

14. Next to each verse list the afflictions Paul suffered for Christ's sake.

Verse 23

Verse 24

Verse 25

Verse 26

Verse 27

Verse 28

It's interesting to note how Paul refers to his sufferings just a few pages earlier in this same letter to the Corinthian Christians. His sufferings are a mere "momentary, light affliction."

Momentary, light affliction is producing for us an eternal weight of glory far beyond all comparison (2 Cor. 4:17).

15. Look again at the afflictions you listed. What would you call them?

16. Verse 29—How do you think Paul's sufferings impacted his ministry to others?

That I may know Him, and the power of His resurrection and the fellowship of His sufferings, being conformed to His death (Phil. 3:10).

17. When you consider that Paul himself wrote the above verse, how does today's passage help you understand what he meant by "the fellowship of His sufferings"?

DAY 3

18. Write your week 5 memory verse ("idolatry").

Read Daniel 3:1-30.

19. Verse 1—What did King **Nebuchadnezzar** do?

20. What were the king's **orders in regard** to his actions? (vv. 4-5)

21. Verse 6—What would happen to the one **who disobeyed these orders?**

22. What were the charges brought by the Chaldeans? (vv. 8,12)

23. What was the king's response? (vv. 13-15)

24. Write your week 21 memory verse ("Faith").

25. What impresses you most about the faith of Shadrach, Meshach, and Abed-nego? (vv. 16-18)

26. What was the king's response to their statement of faith? (v. 19)

27. What action was specifically carried out in regard to Shadrach, Meshach, and Abed-nego? (vv. 20-21)

28. What happened to those who carried them to the furnace? (v. 22)

29. What happened to Shadrach, Meshach, and Abed-nego? (vv. 23-27)

Remember the words of Jesus to His followers in the passage you read yesterday? "Yet not a hair of your head will perish" (Luke 21:18).

30. Just as God was able to use the fire to burn off the ties that bound Shadrach, Meshach, and Abed-nego, how is He able to use the "fiery trials" in your life?

Some think the fourth being in the furnace (v. 25) was a pre-incarnate appearance of Christ. This is called a Theophany.

31. If the king was able to see Christ when Shadrach, Meshach, and Abed-nego were in the furnace, how do you think God is able to use the sufferings in your life in regard to unbelievers?

32. How was God glorified? (vv. 26,28-29)

33. What happened to Shadrach, Meshach, and Abed-nego? (v. 30)

DAY 4

Read 1 Peter 4:1-2,12-19.

It is important to realize what verse 1 is *not* saying. It is *not* saying that whoever suffers ceases to sin. People who suffer still sin. It is also *not* saying that suffering in itself purifies and strengthens people. Some are strengthened, but some become embittered towards God.

"Arm yourselves also with the same purpose" (v. 1). We usually think of suffering as something to arm ourselves against; yet here we are told to arm ourselves with it.

34. What does verse 2 indicate that suffering is an excellent armor against? Why?

35. According to the following verses, how should you react when you encounter suffering?

Verse 12

Verse 13

They took his advice; and after calling the apostles in, they flogged them and ordered them to speak no more in the name of Jesus, and then released them. So they went on their way from the presence of the Council, rejoicing that they had been considered worthy to suffer shame for His name (Acts 5:40-41).

36. Verse 14—If a person suffers for Christ, what is true about her?

37. Verse 16—If a person suffers for Christ, how can she respond?

It is better, if God should will it so, that you suffer for doing what is right rather than for doing what is wrong (1 Pet. 3:17).

38. Verse15—List wrong actions mentioned and how a person might suffer as a result of committing them.

39. How do you think innocent people might become victims of suffering because of these actions?

40. Maybe you have suffered as the result of someone's sin. How can you allow God to use it for good?

41. How can you allow Satan to use it for evil?

42. Is there sin in your life that is causing another to suffer?

43. Verse 19—When trials come, what should you remember about God?

44. When trials come, what should you remember to do?

DAY 5

We have seen in this study how suffering comes as a result of identifying with Christ, righteousness, sin, other people, and ourselves. Today we will look at two other sources of suffering.

Read Job 1:6-22.

45. What did Satan say to God in regard to Job? (vv. 9-11)

"Free will is a gift we would not wish to do without. Yet we wonder why God does not intervene in the exercise of *other* people's free will. Why are *they* allowed to cause wars and misuse resources and make others suffer? Why are poverty, government corruption, tyranny, and injustice permitted to go on and on? Of course it is never our choices that are at stake here; it is other people's. We do not want God to curtail our freedom; we only want him to restrain others."[3]
—Elisabeth Elliot

46. Write your week 11 memory verse ("God's Sovereignty").

47. Verse 12—What did God do?

48. Why is it significant that Satan had to have permission from God to have any power over Job?

49. What did Satan do to Job?

Verses 14-15

Verse 16

Verse 17

Verses 18-19

Read Job 2:1-10.

50. Verse 3—What does the Lord say about Job?

51. What did Satan say in regard to Job? (vv. 4-5)

52. Verse 6—What did God do?

53. Verse 7—What did Satan do to Job?

54. What concepts of God surfaced in Job's life as a result of his sufferings?

Job 1:21

Job 2:10

55. What do Job 1:22 and 2:10 reveal about Job's integrity?

56. Job "fell to the ground and worshiped" (Job 1:20) What example does this set for you in responding to suffering? How is this response possible?

Read Hosea 5:15.

57. Why did God remove the sense of His presence from Israel?

58. What does affliction cause a person to do?

Read Hosea 6:1-3.

59. What is hard for you to accept in regard to God as the cause of suffering?

60. Why does God "tear" and "wound" us?

Just as the sufferings of Christ are ours in abundance, so also our comfort is abundant through Christ (2 Cor. 1:5).

61. Verse 3—What is even more certain than the sufferings we endure?

"More often ... our tears become telescopes through which we more clearly see our God. Truths obscured in the noontime of affluence become clear in the black midnight of suffering. God, who is light, is often found in the darkness."[5]

62. What do you know about God that you would not know if He had not allowed you to suffer?

"You and I obviously do not seek out adversity just so we can develop a deeper relationship with God. Rather God, through adversity, seeks us out. It is God who draws us more and more into a deeper relationship with Him. If we are seeking Him it is because He is seeking us. One of the strong cords with which He draws us into a more intimate, personal relationship with Him is adversity. If, instead of fighting God or doubting Him in times of adversity, we will seek to cooperate with God, we will find that we will be drawn into a deeper relationship with Him."[6]

> "Moments of great spiritual delight do not require much faith; if we never came down from the mount of blessing we might easily come to trust in our own delights rather than in the unshakable character of God. It is necessary therefore that our watchful Heavenly Father withdraw His inward comforts from us sometimes to teach us that Christ alone is the Rock upon which we must repose our everlasting trust."[4]
> —A. W. Tozer

[1]Charles Stanley, *How to Handle Adversity* (Nashville: Thomas Nelson, Publishers Inc., 1989), 24.

[2]Wayne Grudem, *Tyndale New Testament Commentaries, 1 Peter* (Leicester, England: InterVarsity Press/Grand Rapids Michigan: William B. Eerdmans Publishing Company, 1988, 1989), 167.

[3]Elisabeth Elliot, *Trusting God in a Twisted World*, Fleming H. Revell, a division of Baker Book House Company, 1989, 140.

[4]A. W. Tozer, *The Root of the Righteous* (Camp Hill, Pennsylvania: Christian Publications, 1955,1986), 128.

[5]Fred M. Wood, *Hosea: Prophet of Reconciliation* (Nashville: Convention Press, 1975), 36.

[6]*Trusting God*, Jerry Bridges, © 1988.Used by Permission of NavPress/Pinon Press. All rights reserved. For Copies call 1-800-366-7788.

WEEK 23
THE OMNISCIENCE OF GOD

SCRIPTURE MEMORY
God Knows All
■ Psalm 139:1-2
■ Proverbs 15:3
■ Hebrews 4:13

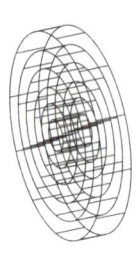

DAY 1

The Omniscience of God is His divine attribute of perfect knowledge. It means that He knows all things. A. W. Tozer writes of God's Omniscience. He says:

"God perfectly knows Himself and, being the source and author of all things, it follows that He knows all that can be known. And this He knows instantly and with a fullness of perfection that includes every possible item of knowledge concerning everything that exists or could have existed anywhere in the universe at any time in the past or that may exist in the centuries or ages yet unborn."

"Because God knows all things perfectly, He knows no thing better than any other thing, but all things equally well. He never discovers anything. He is never surprised, never amazed. He never wonders about anything nor (except when drawing men out for their own good) does He seek information or ask questions."[1]

Read Psalm 147:4-5.

1. Verse 5—How does this verse characterize the omniscience of God?

2. Verse 4—How does the sky testify to the omniscience of God?

Read Job 37:14-16.

3. Verse 16—How does this verse characterize the omniscience of God?

4. How does the weather testify to the omniscience of God? (vv. 15-16)

Read Psalm 50:10-11.

5. How does the animal kingdom testify to the omniscience of God?

Read Hebrews 4:13.

6. How does your existence testify to the omniscience of God?

7. Describe below what God's omniscience means to you.

DAY 2

Read Isaiah 40:12-17.

8. Write what the following words reveal about God's omniscience. (A dictionary may help.)

    director

    instructor

    counselor

    teacher

    informant

9. What are the monumental things listed in verse 12?

10. Yet, who knows the measurements, calculations, and weight of all of the things you just listed?

11. What are the monumental things mentioned in verse 15?

12. Yet, what are they in comparison to God? (vv. 15,17)

"Who has measured the waters in the hollow of His hand" (v. 12). Think about it. God is able to hold all the water that covers the earth in the palm of His hand. Yet, His divine attributes (Love, Compassion, Grace, Omniscience, Immutability, Sovereignty, etc.), are not held in His hand, but rather make up the hand that holds those waters.

13. How does this knowledge impact your concept of God?

Oh, the depth of the riches both of the wisdom and knowledge of God! How unsearchable are His judgments and unfathomable His ways! For who has known the mind of the Lord, or who became His counselor? (Rom. 11:33-34).

"Who has put wisdom in the innermost being, Or has given understanding to the mind?" (Job 38:36).

Read Daniel 2:20-23.

This is a prayer of adoration which Daniel lifts up to the Lord after God reveals to him the dream of King Nebuchadnezzar and its interpretation.

14. Verse 20—Who has ownership of wisdom and power?

15. How does a person come to possess these things? (v. 21)

16. When you consider the present state of the world, how do you feel?

17. Do you think there is anything in the future that would surprise God? Why or why not?

18. List some Christian and secular occupations which would employ "men of understanding." (v. 21)

19. What is the source of their knowledge, whether they recognize it or not?

It is God Himself who is the *Knower* of all things. And He is also the *Revealer* of all things.

20. Verse 22—What does God reveal and know?

21. Why is it significant not only to understand the things revealed, and the things not known, but to know the Revealer and Knower?

22. How does knowing God shed light upon all knowledge and wisdom which you possess?

That their hearts may be encouraged, having been knit together in love, and attaining to all the wealth that comes from the full assurance of understanding, resulting in a true knowledge of God's mystery, that is, Christ Himself, in whom are hidden all the treasures of wisdom and knowledge (Col. 2:2-3).

23. When people hunger for knowledge, for what do they actually hunger?

24. What does this say about the "men of understanding" you listed?

> "Your character is what God knows you to be— your reputation is only what people think you are."[2]
> —David L. Hocking

DAY 4

"Although you wash yourself with lye And use much soap, The stain of your iniquity is before Me," declares the Lord God (Jer. 2:22).

25. What do the following verses reveal that God knows about a person?

Job 11:11

Psalm 44:20-21

Psalm 69:5

Psalm 90:8

Hosea 7:2

A favorite game of infants is "peek-a-boo." Over and over they will cover their face with a blanket, thinking their whole body is hidden from you. Since they can't see you, they think you can't see them.

26. When do we play "peek-a-boo" with God in regard to sin?

27. What do the following verses say in regard to this game?

Proverbs 15:3

Jeremiah 16:17

28. If we are unable to deceive God in regard to the sin in our lives, whom are we actually fooling when we walk through our days as though our sins go unnoticed?

When I kept silent about my sin, my body wasted away Through my groaning all day long. For day and night Thy hand was heavy upon me; My vitality was drained away as with the fever heat of summer. I acknowledged my sin to Thee, And my iniquity I did not hide; I said, "I will confess my transgressions to the Lord"; And Thou didst forgive the guilt of my sin" (Ps. 32:3-5).

The Omniscience of God   **169**

29. What is the purpose of confessing sin before a God who knows everything?

30. What happens when we try to hide our sin from a God who is omniscient?

31. At this moment my heart feels (check one)

 ❑ terrified
 ❑ free
 ❑ sober
 ❑ anxious

32. Is there a sin in your life that you need to acknowledge before God? If yes, do as the psalmist did–confess your sin to Him.

DAY 5

Read 2 Timothy 2:19.

33. Why is the omniscience of God a source of comfort for you?

Read Psalm 33:13-15.

34. What does God see?

He who fashions the hearts of them all, He who understands all their works (v. 15).

35. What is the significance of the word *fashion* in the above verse as it relates to the individual?

36. Write your week 14 memory verse ("God Remembers Your Efforts").

37. What else does God know about you?

38. According to the following passages, how is God's omniscience directed toward the details in your life?

 Psalm 139:1-3

 Matthew 10:29-30

39. Write your week 22 memory verse ("Suffering for Christ").

Read Psalm 142:2-3.

40. Verse 3—How is God's omniscience directed toward the sufferings you experience?

"The Lord never forgets. Circumstances may point to the limited human conclusion that he has forgotten us. It may seem that he has had a lapse of memory about our personal plight or about the perplexities of his people as a whole. But … at the very moment we despair, God is arranging a strategy of extrication. Always beyond our perception of the possible, exceeding the reach of our wildest expectation, God is at work."[5]

41. Write your week 13 memory verse ("Prayer").

42. Verse 2—What is the purpose of declaring your trouble before a God who is omniscient?

"The fact is, God already knows our needs, but that eliminates neither the joy of talking to Him about them nor the need of getting our emotions clarified by talking to God. My greater need may be patience, peace, or trust, not simply receiving the answer to my first request. God's knowledge encourages me to pray, because I know that He knows my real needs."[6]

Read Psalm 37:18 and 1 Corinthians 13:12.

43.Why is God's omniscience a source of great hope for you?

"There is, certainly, great cause for humility in the thought that he sees all the twisted things about me that my fellow humans do not see (and am I glad!), and that he sees more corruption in me than that which I see in myself (which in all conscience, is enough). There is, however, equally great incentive to worship and love God in the thought that, for some unfathomable reason, he wants me as his friend, and desires to be my friend, and has given his Son to die for me in order to realize this purpose."[4]
—J. I. Packer

[1]A. W. Tozer, *The Knowledge of the Holy* (San Francisco: Harper & Row, Publishers, 1961), 62-63.
[2]*The Nature of God in Plain Language*, David L. Hocking, 1984, Word Publishing, Nashville, Tennessee. All rights reserved.
[3]J. I. Packer, *Knowing God* (Downers Grove, Illinois: InterVarsity Press, 1973), 42.
[4]Ibid.
[5]*Lord of the Impossible*, Lloyd John Ogilvie, 1984, Abingdon Press. Used by permission.
[6]*The Nature of God in Plain Language*, David L. Hocking, 138.

This week you should know how to share this much of the "God Is Not a Man" Illustration. You should have your ten verses memorized. You should be able to draw this much on a piece of paper.

God Is Not a Man
(Num. 23:19; 1 Sam. 15:29; 1 Cor. 1:25)

Man		God
Willfully hurts	Lamentations 3:22-23; Psalm 103:8; Matthew 9:36	Compassionate
Remembers failures	Isaiah 43:25; Psalm 103:12; Micah 7:19	Harbors no grudge
Forgets efforts	Hebrews 6:10	Remembers your efforts
Changes	Hebrews 13:8; James 1:17; Isaiah 54:10	Immutable
Is full of sin	1 John 3:5; Hebrews 7:26; Hebrews 4:15	Sinless
Untrustworthy/unfaithful	Psalm 111:7-8; Psalm 89:34; 1 Kings 8:23	Trustworthy/faithful
Loves conditionally	Romans 5:8; 1 John 4:10; Romans 8:38-39	Loves unconditionally
Fallible/undependable	Deuteronomy 31:8	Infallible/dependable
Limited knowledge	Psalm 139:1-2; Hebrews 4:13; Proverbs 15:3	Knows all

God Is Not a Man Illustration, David Stephens *Discovering Who He Is*, (Tulsa: D-Vine Focus, 1989), 1.

WEEK 24
THE WILL OF GOD

DAY 1

Last week we studied the omniscience of God–His perfect knowledge, His identity as the Source of all knowledge and the Revealer of all knowledge. We learned how He is omniscient in regard to people and every single detail of an individual's life. It follows, then, that an Omniscient Creator would also have a specific plan for that individual–one that is unique to every person. You are that individual, and you were brought into existence for a very specific purpose.

1. How do these verses reveal that God has a purpose for your life?

Job 23:10

Psalm 1:6

Psalm 32:8

Psalm 37:18

Read Jeremiah 29:10-14.

2. Verse 11—How is this verse even more specific in revealing that purpose?

The king of Babylon, Nebuchadnezzar, invaded Israel and took some of that nation's "cream of the crop" to serve in his court. They were youth with great potential.

Youths in whom was no defect, who were good-looking, showing intelligence in every branch of wisdom, endowed with understanding, and discerning knowledge (Dan. 1:4).

They had been taken from their home–their country. These are the people to whom Jeremiah is prophesying in this passage.

3. Verse 10—How long were these captives to remain in Babylon?

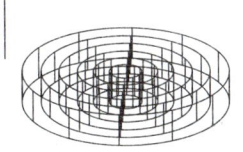

4. What promise would be realized as God's will was carried out? (v. 10)

" 'I know the plans that I have for you' declares the Lord, 'plans for welfare and not for calamity to give you a future and a hope' " (Jer. 29:11).

5. After 70 years in exile what would the people come to realize as their welfare and hope? (vv. 12-13)

6. How would God also minister to their physical needs? (v. 14)

Sometimes we get off-focus when searching for God's will in our lives. We think that it is realized primarily in choosing a college, deciding a career, finding a mate, and so forth. These are important decisions, but they are secondary.

7. What is God's primary will for your life? (vv. 12-13)

8. Then what will follow? (v. 14)

"Seek first His kingdom and His righteousness; and all these things shall be added to you" (Matt. 6:33).

Read Jeremiah 29:4-7.

9. How does this passage reveal that God had a plan for the people within the exile before His ultimate plan was fulfilled? (vv. 10-14)

Simply put, God told them to do what they knew to do-what they had always done; what they would be doing if they were home.

Maybe you feel this time in your life, you are in exile–in a no-man's-land, caught in between childhood and adulthood with no clear vision of God's plan for your life.

But what do you already know to be God's will in regard to lifestyle, witnessing, serving, relationships, integrity, and so forth? Be faithful to do what you know to do, and God will be faithful to reveal to you His ultimate plan for your life.

10. Verse 7—Though Nebuchadnezzar had executed the invasion, Who had actually brought these youth into exile?

11. Who has placed you where you are now?

DAY 2

There is a way which seems right to a man, But its end is the way of death (Prov. 14:12).

12. Why are the following statements inadequate sources in determining God's will?

"I just felt like it was the right thing to do."
"My instincts told me to go for it."
"It just seemed like the logical thing to do."

13. Compare these "two hearts" in regard to determining God's will. What is the difference?

Heart A—"The heart is more deceitful than all else And is desperately sick; Who can understand it?" (Jer. 17:9).

Heart B—Beloved, if our heart does not condemn us, we have confidence before God (1 John 3:21).

You may be thinking, *How do I know when my heart is in a condition to determine God's will?* We'll look for an answer to this question in God's Word.

Read Psalm 37:4.

14. What does it mean to "delight yourself in the Lord?"

According to *Strong's Concordance*, the word *delight* as used in this verse means "to be happy about" or "to make merry over." It's the picture of experiencing "exquisite delight" in God.

We find the same word in Job.

"Then you will delight in the Almighty, And lift up your face to God" (Job 22:26).

15. How does the phrase, "lift up your face to God" shed light on what it means to delight yourself in the Lord?

Read Job 22:26 again. It says, "then you will delight in the Almighty." Let's take a look at the verses that precede this verse to learn when we are delighting in the Almighty.

Read Job 22:21-28.

16. The following verses serve as a check list to help determine whether or not a person delights himself in the Lord. Next to each verse write what it says.

    Verse 21

    Verse 22

    Verse 23

    Verse 24

17. How do the following verses also describe a person who is delighting in the Lord?

    Romans 12:2

    Proverbs 3:5-6

18. Write your week 18 memory verse ("Seeking God").

19. Verse 25—Considering the verse you just wrote, what do you think "the Almighty will be your gold" means?

Beloved, if our heart does not condemn us, we have confidence before God (1 John 3:21).

20. How can a heart that delights itself in the Lord have confidence before God? (vv. 27-28)

    Verse 27

    Verse 28

21. How does this truth relate to knowing God's will for your life?

22. Review today's study. Describe the heart that can be trusted to determine God's will.

Is your heart prepared to lead you in the right path, into God's will for your life? If you can't answer this objectively, find a more mature believer who can help you determine the truth about the condition of your heart.

"I will give you a new heart and put a new spirit within you; and I will remove the heart of stone from your flesh and give you a heart of flesh" (Ezek. 36:26).

When God's desires become your desires, you can trust your heart to lead you in the right path.

DAY 3

23. **The Lord, through His Holy Spirit, reveals His will through the sources listed below. Read the Scriptures on the right and match them with the corresponding source on the left.**

    _____ circumstances   A. Psalm 119:130
    _____ prayer   B. Proverbs 12:15; 15:22
    _____ the Bible   C. John 5:19-20
    _____ the counsel of others   D. James 1:5

God reveals His will through the Bible

24. **Write your week 7 memory verse ("The Bible").**

25. **Look at the verse you just wrote. If you want God to reveal His will to you, why should you turn to the pages in the Bible as opposed to the pages of a career manual, a teen magazine, or any other book?**

God reveals His will through prayer.

26. **Write your week 13 memory verse ("Prayer").**

Read Matthew 26:38-42.

27. **Do you think that Satan's objective in all temptation is to lead a person away from God's will? Explain.**

28. **Verse 39—What evidence is there that Satan was tempting Jesus to oppose the Father's will?**

29. **Verse 38—How did this affect Jesus?**

30. **How are you affected by the thought of missing God's will for your own life?**

31. **Verse 39—What did Jesus do?**

32. What instructions did Jesus give His disciples in regard to temptation?

33. What impact does prayer have on strengthening the flesh's desire to do the will of God? (vv. 39,42)

God reveals His will through circumstances

Read John 5:17.

34. What evidence is there from this verse that God's will can be found in the things that are happening today?

35. In the space below, recall a circumstance in your life that God used to reveal His will to you.

36. What is the danger of trusting in circumstances alone to determine God's will?

God reveals His will through the counsel of godly people

37. Write your week 12 memory verse ("Authority").

38. Answer the following statements by checking the appropriate box:

❑ yes ❑ no ❑ sometimes   I am more apt to give advice than to receive it.

❑ yes ❑ no ❑ sometimes   I seek advice from my parents.

❑ yes ❑ no ❑ sometimes   I seek advice from others more spiritually mature than myself.

❑ yes ❑ no ❑ sometimes   I go to friends my own age and seek their advice before I go to those who are older and wiser than myself.

❑ yes ❑ no ❑ sometimes   I seek advice mostly from people who will tell me what I want to hear.

Morris Ashcraft writes, "One cannot really do the will of God apart from the fellowship of other believers. ... Every Christian should be in regular conversation with other serious believers. ... They see us more clearly than we see ourselves sometimes. ... Serious conversation with other serious Christians is an essential for those who would do the will of God."[3]

39. List names of persons who could form a good spiritual counseling "panel" for you. Do not include names of your peers.

DAY 4

Paul E. Little writes, "The will of God is not like a magic package let down out of heaven by a string, a package we grope after in desperation and hope sometime in the future to clasp to our hearts."

The will of God is far more like a scroll that unrolls every day. In other words, God has a will for you and me today and tomorrow and the next day and the day after that. ... It is not something to be grasped as a package once for all."[4]

40. What part of the scroll has God already unrolled in His Word for you in regard to the following:

Lifestyle (Col. 1:9-10)

Relationships (2 Cor. 6:14)

Ministry (Matt. 28:19)

Work (Eph. 6:5-6)

41. What else has God revealed to you?

There are obviously many issues which are black and white in determining the will of God. The Ten Commandments is one example. But what about the gray areas, the ones which are not so clear?

42. Can you think of a specific "gray area" to which each of the following Scriptures could help give direction? Write examples or situations next to each verse.

1 Corinthians 6:12

1 Corinthians 6:19-20

1 Corinthians 8:9

1 Corinthians 10:31

43. What is an area in your life in which you are at a crossroad?

44. How does Scripture help you to see the truth more clearly in regard to this area?

45. What fears do you have in doing the will of God?

46. What do these fears reveal to you about your concept of Him?

Read Psalm 16:7-11.

47. What evidence do you find that David had sought the will of the Lord? (vv. 7-8)

48. According to these verses, what are the blessings for the one who seeks to do the will of God?

Verse 9

Verse 10

Verse 11

In peace I will both lie down and sleep, For Thou alone, O Lord, dost make me to dwell in safety (Ps. 4:8).

49. What have you learned about God through this study that convinces your heart that He knows what is best for your life?

[1] *On the Anvil*, Max Lucado © 1985. Used by permission of Tyndale House Publishers, Inc. All rights reserved.
[2] Henry Blackaby and Claude V. King, *Experiencing God Knowing and Doing the Will of God, Youth Edition* (Nashville: LifeWay Press, 1994), 103.
[3] Morris Ashcraft, *The Will of God* (Nashville: Broadman Press, 1980), 137.
[4] Paul Little, *Affirming the Will of God*, InterVarsity Press, 1971, 137.

THE ETERNITY OF GOD

DAY 1

SCRIPTURE MEMORY
God Gives Eternal Life
- John 5:24
- John 6:40
- John 11:25-26

1. Describe how the following verses express the eternal nature of God the Creator.

Job 36:26

Psalm 9:7

Psalm 93:2

Revelation 1:8

2. Describe how the following verses express the temporal nature of human beings.

Job 7:7

Psalm 39:5

Psalm 89:48

James 4:14

3. When you compare these two sets of verses, what is it about the eternal nature of God that draws you to Him?

As evidenced by our pursuit of outer space, humans are drawn to eternity. Scientists continue to develop technology that will allow us to see our solar system and beyond. It seems to have no beginning or end, and we don't even know that for certain.

But one thing we do know: there is more, *much more* beyond what our technology lets us see. Even if we were to look at the earth from the position of the moon, we would see that in all directions the earth has its beginning and ending in space–a planet suspended in the middle of what appears to be eternity.

C. S. Lewis illustrates it like this: "If you picture Time as a straight line along which we have to travel, then you must picture God as the whole page on which the line is drawn. We come to the parts of the line one by one: we have to leave A behind before we get to B, and cannot reach C until we leave B behind. God, from above or outside or all round, contains the whole line, and sees it all."[1]

J. Wallace Hamilton also gives us a helpful illustration in understanding time in light of the eternal God. He writes, "You and I are very much like small boys trying to see a circus parade through a knothole in the fence. All we can see through our little knothole is the present, that which is happening now. That part of the parade which has gone by is the past. We cannot see the past; we can only remember it and not very well. That part of the parade yet to come is the future. We cannot see that at all, not even a day of it. All we can grasp through our little knothole is the now—this moment, this experience of pain or pleasure. And we are strongly inclined to judge the whole show by that, by what is happening to us now."

"It is part of what we mean by the omniscience and the omnipresence of God. He is above the fence. To Him there is no past or present or future. He is the timeless one. He sees the whole parade. He knows where it began and where it is coming out. And He sees the relation of this moment to the total purpose."[2]

4. When you think about these illustrations, what perspective does the Eternal God have of your life?

DAY 2

Read Psalm 90:1-17.

5. Verse 1—What is the dwelling place of past generations, this generation, and future generations?

6. Verse 2—What has a "birthday"?

7. Verse 2—What indicates that God does not have a birthday?

Do not let this one fact escape your notice, beloved, that with the Lord one day is as a thousand years, and a thousand years as one day (2 Pet. 3:8).

8. What is God's perspective of time?

9. In meditating upon the eternity of God, what perspective did the writer of this psalm acquire about life lived as a human being?

    Verse 3

    Verse 9

    Verse 10

10. The psalmist compares the lives of "children of men" with grass. What observations can you see in this comparison? (vv. 3-6)

11. Verse 12—When the writer meditated upon the eternity of God, what did he come to realize as the value of time here on earth?

12. Verse 10—What is indicated as not being worthy of the time of the person who lives life focused on Eternal God?

13. What will bring a sense of satisfaction to our lives on this earth?

    Verse 14

    Verse 16

    Verse 17

"Lord, make me to know my end, And what is the extent of my days. Let me know how transient I am" (Ps. 39:4).

DAY 3

Read Psalm 102:18-28.

14. Verse 23—How does the psalmist characterize the temporal nature of man?

> "We who live in this nervous age would be wise to meditate on our lives and our days long and often before the face of God and on the edge of eternity. For we are made for eternity as certainly as we are made for time, and as responsible moral beings we must deal with both."[3]
> —A. W. Tozer

He has weakened my strength in the way (Ps 102:23).

> "When we go as far back as possible in our minds (the vanishing point of the past) and step off, there is God. And when we project ourselves to the vanishing point of the future, the misty infinity of tomorrow, again there is our God."[4]
> —Charles R. Swindoll

15. Recall a time when you were weakened physically through either stress, illness, or injury. How does this experience confirm that your existence here on earth is a temporary one?

16. Write your week 15 memory verse ("God Is Immutable").

17. The psalmist compares the earth and the heavens to a garment and clothing. What do you observe in this comparison? (vv. 25-26)

18. How does the psalmist characterize the eternal nature of God?

    Verse 24

    Verse 26

    Verse 27

19. Verse 20—How does death make us a "groaning prisoner?"

20. What is the difference between the children written about in verse 28 and those written about in verse 20?

The last enemy that will be abolished is death (1 Cor. 15:26).

"O death, where is your victory? O death, where is your sting?" The sting of death is sin, and the power of sin is the law; but thanks be to God who gives us the victory through our Lord Jesus Christ (1 Cor. 15:55-57).

21. When you look at these verses from 1 Corinthians and recall what you know about Christ's gospel, why is Jesus the hope for the people written about in both Psalm 102:20 and Psalm 102:28?

22. Verse 18—How are you a fulfillment of the prophecy written in this verse?

Tomorrow we will continue to look at the victory over death which is ours in Christ and the eternal life which is God's gift to us through Jesus.

DAY 4

Read 1 Corinthians 15:1-8,12-22.

23. What is true about Jesus? (vv. 3-4)

24. As proof of His resurrection, to whom did Christ appear after He arose from the grave?

Verse 5

Verse 6

Verse 7

Verse 8

25. What is the significance of Christ's resurrection in regard to ...

The truthfulness of the gospel (vv. 14-15,17).

Those who have died (v. 18).

The future hope of our resurrection (vv. 19-20).

26. What did Adam pass on to all of mankind? (vv. 21-22)

27. What does Christ pass on to those who are His?

Jesus said to her, "I am the resurrection and the life; he who believes in Me shall live even if he dies, and everyone who lives and believes in Me shall never die. Do you believe this?" (John 11:25-26).

Read John 8:58.

28. How does Jesus express His eternal nature in this verse?

Read John 5:21-29.

29. What do the following verses say about God the Father, and Jesus, the Son?

Verse 21

Verse 24

Verse 26

30. What has the Father given to the Son? (vv. 22,27)

31. Yet, how may a person escape this? (v. 24)

"This is the will of My Father, that everyone who beholds the Son and believes in Him, may have eternal life; and I Myself will raise him up on the last day" (John 6:40).

32. Verse 29—What are eternity's two options?)

33. How will this be initiated? (vv. 25,28)

Dealing out retribution to those who do not know God and to those who do not obey the gospel of our Lord Jesus. And these will pay the penalty of eternal destruction, away from the presence of the Lord and from the glory of His power (2 Thess. 1:8-9).

34. How is eternity described in 2 Thessalonians 1:8-9?

35. For whom has this side of eternity been prepared?

36. As you think through this passage and its truths, what are your thoughts toward nonbelievers you know?

DAY 5

Read John 10:24-30.

37. Jesus told the Jews who had gathered around Him that they were not of His sheep. What did He say was the reason for this? (vv. 25-26)

38. What three things does Jesus say characterize His sheep? (v. 27)

39. What is their reward? (v. 28)

40. Which of the following best represents the picture of salvation Jesus describes in verse 28. (check one)

   ❏ It's a picture of my grip or hold on God.
   ❏ It's a picture of God's grip or hold on me.

41. With this picture in mind, what does verse 28 indicate can pry open this grip?

42. What does this guarantee in your relationship to the Father? (v. 29)

43. According to verses 28-29 what kind of "grip" are you in?

Hence, also, He is able to save forever those who draw near to God through Him, since He always lives to make intercession for them (Heb. 7:25).

[1] *Mere Christianity* by C. S. Lewis copyright © C. S. Lewis Pte. Ltd. 1942, 1943, 1944, 1952. Extract reprinted by permission.
[2] J. Wallace Hamilton, *Who Goes There? What and Where Is God?* (Old Tappan: Revell Company, 1958), 123.
[3] A. W. Tozer, *The Knowledge of the Holy* (San Francisco: Harper & Row Publishers, 1961), 47.
[4] *Living Above the Level of Mediocrity: A Commitment to Excellence,* Charles R. Swindoll, 1987 Word Publishing, Nashville, Tennessee. All rights reserved.

This week you should know how to share this much of the "God Is Not a Man" Illustration. You should have your eleven verses memorized. You should be able to draw this much on a piece of paper.

God Is Not a Man
(Num. 23:19; 1 Sam. 15:29; 1 Cor. 1:25)

Man		God
Willfully hurts	Lamentations 3:22-23; Psalm 103:8; Matthew 9:36	Compassionate
Remembers failures	Isaiah 43:25; Psalm 103:12; Micah 7:19	Harbors no grudge
Forgets efforts	Hebrews 6:10	Remembers your efforts
Changes	Hebrews 13:8; James 1:17; Isaiah 54:10	Immutable
Is full of sin	1 John 3:5; Hebrews 7:26; Hebrews 4:15	Sinless
Untrustworthy/unfaithful	Psalm 111:7-8; Psalm 89:34; 1 Kings 8:23	Trustworthy/faithful
Loves conditionally	Romans 5:8; 1 John 4:10; Romans 8:38-39	Loves unconditionally
Fallible/undependable	Deuteronomy 31:8	Infallible/dependable
Limited knowledge	Psalm 139:1-2; Hebrews 4:13; Proverbs 15:3	Knows all
Dies	John 5:24; John 11:25-26; John 6:40	Eternal

God Is Not a Man Illustration, David Stephens *Discovering Who He Is*, (Tulsa: D-Vine Focus, 1989), 1.

WEEK 26
METHODS OF BIBLE STUDY (1 JOHN)

This week you will study the Book of 1 John using one or more of the four methods of Bible study introduced in week 8: Ready, Aim, Fire Method; The P's and Q's Method; The Triple S Method; The John 15:5 Method. You may want to refer to week 8 for an example of each method.

SCRIPTURE MEMORY
Scripture Memory
■ **Job 22:22**
■ **Psalm 119:11**
■ **Psalm 119:42**

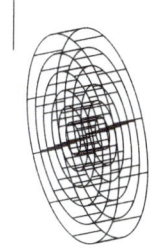

Ready, Aim, Fire Method

Ready—_Bring the principles into focus._ Write points or facts the passage reveals.

Aim—_Finding the target._ What verse stands out to you most?

Fire—_What does my "target verse" challenge me to do?_ How can I put into practice what this verse is saying? What specific commitment do I need to make to live out the truth of this verse?

The P's and Q's Method

P's–_Principles._ Write down the principles the passage teaches.

Q's–_Questions._ Answer the following questions in regard to the principles you discovered in the passage.

What sin do I need to confess?

What example do I need to model?

What command do I need to obey?

Application. Upon answering the questions, what action do I need to take?

The Triple S Method

Standard—State the principle or ideal expressed from one particular verse.

Struggles—How am I not measuring up to this (ideal or principle) in my life?

Strategy—My course of action to change this. How can I apply the Scripture to my problem?

The John 15:5 Method

1. "I am the Vine"—What does this passage reveal about God or Jesus Christ?
2. "You are the branches"—What does this passage reveal about me?
3. "He who abides in Me and I in Him bears much fruit"–What verse from this passage is the Holy Spirit using to prune me so that His fruit can be produced in my life?
4. "For apart from Me you can do nothing"—Pray the following:

Lord, I realize that the first step in applying this truth in my life is to admit that without You I cannot do it. So, I give this to You right now and thank You that no matter what happens, You have taken it. Let me not listen to the voice of the deceiver, who wants me to feel defeated. Let me not trust in my own strength and try to accomplish this in my flesh. But may I place my hope and my trust in You that through Jesus You can accomplish this in me. Amen.

It is important to be specific in your applications. Below are examples of applications for Galatians 6:2, "Bear one another's, burdens and thus fulfill the law of Christ."

Okay: "I will help others more."

Good: "I will be sensitive to someone in need and make myself available to them."

Better: "My mom has had a heavy workload lately so I will bear her burden by helping more around the house."

Best: "God is specifically leading me through this verse to help my mom more around the house since she has had a lot of stress at work. I will do the dishes all week without being asked (whether my brother does his share or not). I will take my brother to soccer practice."

Prove yourselves doers of the word, and not merely hearers who delude themselves (Jas. 1:22).

DAY 1

Ready, Aim, Fire Method
1 John 1

Ready—Bring the principles into focus.

Aim—Finding the target.

Fire—What does my "target verse" challenge me to do?

DAY 2

The P's and Q's Method
1 John 2

P's–_Principles_

Q's–_Questions_

What sin do I need to confess?

What example do I need to model?

What command do I need to obey?

Application

The Triple S Method
1 John 3

Standard

Struggles

Strategy

DAY 4

The John 15:5 Method
1 John 4

1. "I am the Vine"—What is this saying about God or Jesus Christ?

2. "You are the branches"—What does this passage reveal about me?

3. "He who abides in Me and I in Him bears much fruit"—What verse from this passage is the Holy Spirit using to prune me so that His fruit can be produced in my life?

4. "For apart from Me you can do nothing"—Pray the following.

Lord, I realize that the first step in applying this truth in my life is to admit that without You I cannot do it. So, I give this to You right now and thank You that no matter what happens, You have taken it. Let me not listen to the voice of the deceiver, who wants me to feel defeated. Let me not trust my own strength and try to accomplish this in my flesh. But may I place my hope and my trust in You that through Jesus You can accomplish all things in me. Amen.

DAY 5

Have fun doing your Bible study today. Check one of the following four Bible study methods and apply it to the Scripture passage provided.

❏ **Ready, Aim, Fire Method**
❏ **The P's and Q's Method**
❏ **The Triple S Method**
❏ **The John 15:5 Method**

1 John 5

WEEK 27
GAINING AN ETERNAL PERSPECTIVE

DAY 1

SCRIPTURE MEMORY
Eternal Perspective
■ Matthew 6:19-20
■ 2 Corinthians 4:16
■ Philippians 3:20

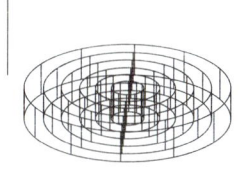

Perspective relates to the way in which people view things. When a person loses perspective of something, it means that his view has become distorted, out of proportion, or lop-sided.

To gain an *eternal* perspective simply means that we see things (life, death, trials, people, time, etc.) the way God sees them. It also relates to our sense of value. God's value system becomes our value system. We value what He values. This study will help define what is most valuable to God, *His* perspective on blessings and trials. And it will also expose the things in our lives of which we have a distorted view.

Read Matthew 6:19-21.

1. Verse 19—What security can earthly treasures promise? Explain.

2. Verse 20—What security do heavenly treasures promise? Explain.

Think about it ...
What can rob you of your joy when heaven *is* your joy?
What can rob you of your peace when heaven *is* your peace?
What can rob you of goodness when heaven *is* your goodness?
What can rob you of delight if heaven *is* your delight?

He shall be the stability of your times, A wealth of salvation, wisdom, and knowledge; The fear of the Lord is his treasure (Isa. 33:6).

3. When you look at the type of treasures you've accumulated, what do they reveal about the true you?

4. When you look at the things you make time for, what is revealed about what you treasure?

5. Verse 21—What one word does Jesus use to describe the person who stores up treasure in heaven?

6. Verse 21—What three things characterize the person whose treasure is in heaven?

7. How is this possible? (See John 15:5.)

Read John 14:1-3.

8. Who is preparing eternity for you even now?

9. How is this eternity described? (vv. 2-3)

"Sell your possessions and give to charity; make yourselves purses which do not wear out, an unfailing treasure in heaven, where no thief comes near, nor moth destroys" (Luke 12:33).

It's interesting how Jesus makes reference not only to the treasures we have but also to the thing that holds those treasures. Consider your purse or wallet. It holds your money, credit cards, pictures of special people, your keys, even your movie rental card. But eventually it will no longer be able to do the job of protecting those treasures. Even brand new, it is not safe from the thief. Perhaps it has not been too long since you asked someone you trusted, "Could you watch my purse for a second?"

10. What significance is there for you that Jesus holds your heavenly treasures and watches over them?

11. What is the difference between an eternal perspective toward material things and the world's perspective toward them?

DAY 2

Read Philippians 3:17-21.

I have told you often before, and I say it again now with tears in my eyes, there are many who walk along the Christian road who are really enemies of the cross of Christ. Their future is eternal loss, for their god is their appetite: they are proud of what they should be ashamed of; and all they think about is this life here on earth (Phil. 3:18-19, TLB).

12. What becomes of the person who claims to know Christ, yet continues to hold on to a worldly perspective? (vv.18-19)

13. How does a worldly perspective make itself known? (v. 19)

14. What is the real truth in regard to them? (v. 18)

15. Write your week 1 memory verse ("The Lordship of Christ").

16. As true followers of Jesus, what should we "keep in mind"? (v. 20)

17. How will this affect your lifestyle?

18. Write your week 25 memory verse ("God Gives Eternal Life").

19. How is your present body described in Philippians 3:21?

20. How is the believer's future body described?

21. Which body is eternal?

DAY 3

He said to them, "You are those who justify yourselves in the sight of men, but God knows your hearts; for that which is highly esteemed among men is detestable in the sight of God" (Luke 16:15).

22. Why will Christ's perspective and the world's perspective always clash?

Read Mark 9:33-37.

23. Verse 34—What was on the hearts of the disciples?

24. Verse 35—Why do you think Jesus' response might have surprised the disciples?

25. How did Jesus characterize greatness? (vv. 36-37)

26. How is this different from the world's concept of greatness?

Read Mark 10:13-16.

27. Verse 13—Had the disciples learned the lesson in Capernaum (recorded in Mark 9:33-37)? Explain.

28. Verse 14—What was Jesus' response?

29. From your perceptions of these passages, how did the disciples view children?

30. What other types of people would be viewed by the world in the same way that the disciples viewed the children?

31. How do you think Jesus responds to these people?

32. What do Jesus' words and actions in these passages teach us about the kingdom of God?

Max Lucado calls it "ugly religion." "When we think God is too busy for little people or too formal for poor protocol. When people are refused access to Christ by those closest to him, the result is empty, hollow religion." Max goes on to write, "It happens when a church spends more time discussing the style of its sanctuary than it does the needs of the hungry. It happens when the brightest minds of the church occupy themselves with dull controversies rather than majestic truths. It happens when a church is known more for its stance on an issue than its reliance upon God."[2]

DAY 4

Read Psalm 49:5-20.

33. What characterizes a worldly perspective?

Verse 6

Verse 11

Verse 18

34. What does the Bible say about those people who live by a worldly perspective?

Verse 12

Verse 13

Verse 17

35. **Why are worldly pursuits unable to fool a person with an eternal perspective?**

    Verse 10

    Verse 14

    Verses 18-19

36. **What is the most priceless treasure on this earth? Why? (vv. 7-9)**

37. **What do you think prevents us from seeing the value of this treasure?**

38. **Read the following situation and then answer the questions that follow.**

    Linda and Marsha are sisters. Linda asks to borrow Marsha's sweater. Marsha refuses, saying, "The last time you wore one of my sweaters, you got a stain on it."

    Is Marsha communicating to Linda that her clothes are more important to her than her own sister?

    Do you see a demonstration of an eternal perspective in Marsha? Explain?

39. **Read the following situation and then answer the questions that follow.**

    Cal and Wayne have grown up together competing academically; though they have remained good friends. Recently, Wayne was able to introduce Cal to Christ, and a new depth to their friendship has been added. With graduation on the horizon, they find themselves competing again–this time for the title of valedictorian. They are neck and neck. It has come down to a single chemistry test. Wayne, with the higher score, edges out Cal. After graduation, Cal learns that Wayne cheated on the test to become valedictorian.

    Though Wayne may have "won," what did he actually lose?

    How might Wayne's actions have been different had he viewed the whole situation through an eternal perspective?

> "What matters most in life is not what ladders we climb or what ownings we accumulate. What matters most is a relationship."[3]
> —Max Lucado

40. How will an eternal perspective on your part impact all of your relationships?

DAY 5

41. Write your week 22 memory verse ("Suffering for Christ").

Read 2 Corinthians 4:16-18.

42. Verse 16—What is true about our outer man?

43. What is true about our inner man?

44. Verse 18—What is described as temporal?

45. What is described as eternal?

46. How are things like acne, lack of a social life, being second string, abuse, loneliness, and so forth described in verse 17?

47. Yet, what is God able to do with these things?

48. Think of a situation where you felt afflicted. Maybe someone hurt your feelings. Maybe someone rejected you. Maybe someone beat you out of a reward for which you worked hard. Briefly describe the situation below.

49. Now, referring to this situation, answer the following questions:

Why would God allow such affliction in your life? (v. 17))

Looking back can you see anything that God may have taught you through this? If yes, what?

So, why can you embrace this affliction? (v. 17)

50. When is it possible for you to prevent your afflictions from producing an "eternal weight of glory"?

51. After completing today's study what do you think having an eternal perspective means in regard to ...

Suffering (Rom. 8:18)

Life (Phil. 1:21,24)

Death (Phil. 1:21,23)

"Life, people, circumstances will press on us what seems to be evil, but God will use it for good to bring us closer to his dream for us."[4]
—Lloyd John Ogilvie

This week you should know how to share this much of the "God Is Not a Man" Illustration. You should have your twelve verses memorized. You should be able to draw this much on a piece of paper. It is important that you understand that God became a man in the Person of His Son, not only to save us from our sins but also as a revelation of His nature. This is something you should be able to communicate as you share this illustration. Though. God is not like man He *became* a man so that we could understand and know Him.

God Is Not a Man
(Num. 23:19; 1 Sam. 15:29; 1 Cor. 1:25)

Man		God
Willfully hurts	Lamentations 3:22-23; Psalm 103:8; Matthew 9:36	Compassionate
Remembers failures	Isaiah 43:25; Psalm 103:12; Micah 7:19	Harbors no grudge
Forgets efforts	Hebrews 6:10	Remembers your efforts
Changes	Hebrews 13:8; James 1:17; Isaiah 54:10	Immutable
Is full of sin	1 John 3:5; Hebrews 7:26; Hebrews 4:15	Sinless
Untrustworthy/unfaithful	Psalm 111:7-8; Psalm 89:34; 1 Kings 8:23	Trustworthy/faithful
Loves conditionally	Romans 5:8; 1 John 4:10; Romans 8:38-39	Loves unconditionally
Fallible/undependable	Deuteronomy 31:8	Infallible/dependable
Limited knowledge	Psalm 139:1-2; Hebrews 4:13; Proverbs 15:3	Knows all
Dies	John 5:24; John 11:25-26; John 6:40	Eternal

God became man in the Person of Jesus Christ as a revelation of His nature.

Jesus Christ
John 1:14; Colossians 1:15; Hebrews 1:3

God Is Not a Man Illustration, David Stephens *Discovering Who He Is*, (Tulsa: D-Vine Focus, 1989), 1.

WEEK 28
JESUS CHRIST, GOD THE SON

DAY 1

SCRIPTURE MEMORY
Jesus Christ
■ **John 1:14**
■ **Colossians 1:15**
■ **Hebrews 1:3**

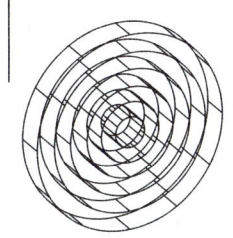

If a person wants to discover who Jesus is, the Gospel of John is an excellent place to begin his or her search. The writer records many of the simple comparisons that Jesus used to reveal Himself.

1. Next to each verse and title write what is revealed about Jesus.

John 3:16 "Begotten Son"

John 4:10,13-14 "Living Water"

John 6:35,48 "Bread of Life"

John 8:12 "The Light of the World"

John 10:9 "The Door"

John 10:11 "The Good Shepherd"

John 11:25 "The Resurrection"

John 13:13 "Teacher" and "Lord"

John 14:6 "The Way, the Truth and the Life"

John 15:5 "The Vine"

2. Write your week 18 memory verse ("Seeking God").

3. If a person is seeking God, why will he or she find Him in Jesus?

4. What can your physical appetites (thirst, hunger, etc.) teach you about your spiritual appetites?

If persons were thirsty, Jesus said, "I am the Living Water." If they were facing death He said, "I am the Resurrection." If they needed security, He said, "I am the Good Shepherd." and "I am the Light." Regardless of all the things we think that we need, Jesus says, "You need Me."

5. Compare your need for air to breathe with your need for Jesus.

Read John 8:23.

6. What does Jesus say to reveal that He is different from mankind?

God so loved the world, that He gave His only begotten Son, that whoever believes in Him should not perish, but have eternal life (John 3:16).

"God created man in His own image, in the image of God He created him; male and female He created them" (Gen. 1:27).

In these two familiar verses, we see what sets Jesus apart from every human being on earth, past, present, and future. The key to understanding this difference is in two words: "begotten" and "created."

7. What is the difference between something that is born and something that is made?

C. S. Lewis helps us understand this. He writes, "To beget is to become the father of; to create is to make. And the difference is this. When you beget, you beget something of the same kind as yourself. A man begets human babies, a beaver begets little beavers and a bird begets eggs which turn into little birds. But when you make, you make something of a different kind from yourself. A bird makes a nest, a beaver builds a dam, a man makes a wireless set—or he may make something more like himself than a wireless set: say a statue. If he is a clever carver he may make a statue which is very much like a man indeed. But, of course, it is not a real man; it only looks like one. It cannot breathe or think. It is not alive."

"What God begets is God; just as what man begets is man. What God creates is not God; just as what man makes is not man. That is why men are not Sons of God in the sense that Christ is. They may be like God in certain ways, but they are not things of the same kind. They are more like statues or pictures of God."[1]

Let's look at some verses that confirm the fact that Jesus is begotten of God—that He is God.

8. Write your week 16 memory verse ("Christ Is Sinless").

9. Write how the following verses also reveal that Christ is sinless.

Matthew 26:28

Mark 2:5

John 8:46

10. "Omnipotence" is the divine attribute which characterizes that God is all powerful. Match each verse to the specific power of God.

_____ Luke 4:39   A. Power over death.
_____ Luke 7:14-15; 8:54-55   B. Power over nature.
_____ Mark 4:35-41   C. Power over demons.
_____ Luke 4:35-36   D. Power over disease.

11. Write your week 23 memory verse ("God Knows All").

12. Match the following verses which reveal Jesus' omniscience to the specific things He knew listed on the right.

_____ John 4:16-19   A. Secret history.
_____ Mark 2:8   B. Secret thoughts of men.
_____ John 6:64   C. All things.
_____ Luke 5:4-6   D. All aspects of the future.
_____ John 16:30   E. Judas would betray Him.

13. Of the things we looked at today, which is the most helpful in confirming in your heart that Jesus is God? Why?

DAY 3

Read John 1:1-5,14-18.

14. What are the purposes of words?

In the beginning was the Word (John 1:1).

15. How does verse 2 reveal that "the Word" is a person?

16. Jesus is "The Word" written of in verse 1. How do the following verses express His deity—that He is God?

Verse 1

Verse 3

17. Why is Jesus referred to as "the Word"?

"As the first apostles looked back in the light of their companionship with the risen Christ ... They said that Jesus *was* the voice of God ... which said at Creation, 'Let there be light!' which divided the waters of the Red Sea, which spoke through the mouths of the prophets and which whispers in the conscience of man—that eternal voice of God became not only audible but visible in Jesus Christ and once for all declared itself in a language that all men can understand."[2]

18. Write your week 25 memory verse ("God Gives Eternal Life").

The darkness did not comprehend it (John 1:5).

The darkest room cannot overpower the smallest flicker of light. Yet, the light that we experience in the physical sense is not eternal. The sun sets, the moon is hidden behind the clouds, a light bulb burns out, and so forth.

In Him was life, and the life was the light of men (v.4).

19. What does Jesus' light allow us to understand?

Verse 14

Verse 16

Verse 17

Thy word is a lamp to my feet, And a light to my path (Ps. 119:105).

20. How does Jesus' life in you light your path?

21. Jesus, the True Light, reveals the truth of God's nature. Write a "T" beside the statements that are revealed through the True Light. Write an "F" beside the statements that reveal a false light.

_____ God's love is unconditional, unchanging, and never-ending.
_____ God is unknowable.
_____ If God is present, you will feel it.
_____ God understands and accepts the sins of teenagers, knowing that they will grow out of them.
_____ God forgives all sins of the Christian.
_____ Everything, good or bad, happens only because God has given permission for it to happen.
_____ God shows favoritism.

22. Why do you think that a person will be unable to find contentment in the darkness?

The Word became flesh (v. 14).

Reflect on the following awe-inspiring thoughts as you consider the miracle of God becoming flesh in the person of Jesus, God the Son.

God made a personal visit to the earth in the person of Jesus Christ. He took on flesh. Jesus was as much divine as if He had never been man and as much man as if He had never been God. He is the God-man. Have you ever thought about what it meant for God to become man?

"God as a fetus. Holiness sleeping in a womb. The creator of life being created. God was given eyebrows, elbows, two kidneys and a spleen. He stretched against the walls and floated in the amniotic fluids of his mother. God had come near."[4]

"... the supreme mystery with which the gospel confronts us, does not lie ... in the Good Friday message of atonement, nor in the Easter message of resurrection, but in the Christmas message of incarnation. ... 'The Word was made flesh' (John 1:14); God became man; the divine Son became a Jew; the Almighty appeared on earth as a helpless human baby, unable to do more than lie and stare and wriggle and make noises, needing to be fed and changed and taught to talk like any other child ..."

"It is not strange that he, the Author of life, should rise from the dead. If he was truly God the Son, it is much more startling that he should die than that he should rise again."[5]

"He who had known the ceaseless worship of angels came to be a slave to men. Preaching, teaching, healing the sick, and raising the dead were parts of His ministry, of course, and the parts we might consider ourselves willing to do for God if that is what He asked. He could be *seen to be God* in those. But Jesus also walked miles in the dusty heat. He healed, and people forgot to thank Him. He was pressed and harried by mobs of exigent people, got tired and thirsty and hungry, was 'tailed' and watched and pounced upon by suspicious, jealous, self-righteous leaders, and in the end was flogged and spat on and stripped and had nails hammered through His hands. He relinquished the right (or the honor) of being publicly treated as equal with God."[6]

23. Describe your thoughts as you reflect on Jesus as God the Son.

DAY 4

Titles reveal a lot about a person. Just think of the images that come to your mind as you read the following titles. The Heavy Weight Champion of the World; Miss America; The Queen of England; The President of the United States.

> "Jesus was not human in the sense of being flawed. He shows us humanity as we were meant to be. He shows us what humanity looks like without sin, and it is breathtaking and marvelous."[3]
> —Rebecca Manley Pippert

We can learn much of what Jesus reveals to us simply by understanding some of the names or titles used to distinguish Him. Meditate on the following list as you contemplate what these names reveal about Jesus.

Alpha and Omega	Chief Cornerstone
First born	King of Kings
Savior of the world	Wonderful
Counselor	Everlasting Father
Arm of the Lord	Prince of peace
Bright Morning Star	Ruler
Rose of Sharon	Lamb of God
Mighty God	Teacher

In our very first study, week 1, we learned what is ascribed to Jesus Christ with the title of "Lord." This title not only applies to His Lordship over all creation but also to His Lordship in our individual lives.

Jesus' favorite way of identifying Himself was The Son of Man. In understanding that Jesus is the God-man, it might be natural to conclude that He is identifying Himself with humanity when using the self-designation of Son of Man. In the same way, we might think that when the Bible refers to Him as the Son of God that it is referring to His deity. Indeed, the Son of Man does bring an element of humility with it. But let's look at how the role of "The Son of Man" is revealed in the following verses.

24. Write what each verse reveals is the function of the "Son of Man."

Matthew 25:31-33

Mark 2:28

Luke 5:24

John 3:13

25. Does what you wrote emphasize Jesus' humanity or deity? Explain.

Read Daniel 7:9-10.

26. Describe how The Ancient of Days is characterized.

Read Revelation 1:12-16 and 5:11-12.

27. Describe how The Son of Man is characterized.

28. What do you find to be similar in these two descriptions?

These Scriptures undeniably give us a portrait of the deity of the Son of Man.

Read Mark 10:45.

29. What is the function of the Son of Man?

Think about it. Jesus, the Son of Man has "myriads, and thousands of thousands" tending to Him in worship and praise night and day. Yet, you are served by the One who is served by the myriads and the thousands.

30. What does this fact reveal about Jesus, and what does it reveal about you?

> "Christ walked with men on earth that He might show them what God is like and make known the true nature of God to a race that had wrong ideas about Him. This was only one of the things He did while here in the flesh, but this He did with beautiful perfection."[8]
> —A. W. Tozer

DAY 5

Read Hebrews 1:1-14.

31. Verse 1—How did God speak to the people of the Old Testament?

32. From your own observations, how do you think the people of the Old Testament viewed God?

33. Verse 2—How did God speak to the people in the New Testament?

34. What does verse 2 say about Jesus?

35. Verse 3—Why can we know what God is like by looking to Jesus?

36. What do you know about God that you would not know if Jesus had not come to the earth?

He is the image of the invisible God, the first-born of all creation (Col. 1:15).

Having become as much better than the angels (Heb. 1:4).

The Jews boasted that their law had been given at Sinai by angels. (See Gal. 3:19.) Therefore, they presumed that the law given to Moses would continue forever. But the writer of Hebrews declares that Jesus, the mediator of a new covenant, is greater than the angels.

37. **Write what God the Father says about God the Son according to the following verses in Hebrews 1.**

Verse 5

Verse 6

Verse 8

Verse 9

Verse 13

38. **Though Jesus is on the throne ruling with His righteous scepter, what are the angels doing? (vv. 7-8)**

39. **Write your week 15 memory verse ("God Is Immutable").**

40. **According to the following verses, what does God the Father say about the Son to establish His Immutability? (Refer to week 15.)**

Verse 11

Verse 12

---

[1]*Mere Christianity* by C. S. Lewis copyright © C. S. Lewis Pte. Ltd. 1942, 1943, 1944, 1952. Extract reprinted by permission.

[2]*God in Man's Experience,* Leonard Griffith, 1968, Word Publishing, Nashville, Tennessee. All rights reserved.

[3]Rebecca Manley Pippert, *Hope Has Its Reasons* (San Francisco: Harper & Row Publishers, 1989), 101.

[4]Max Lucado, *God Came Near* (Portland, Multnomah Press, 1987), 25-26.

[5]J. I. Packer, *Knowing God* (Downers Grove, Illinois: InterVarsity Press, 1973), 54.

[6]Elisabeth Elliot, *Discipline: The Glad Surrender,* Fleming H. Revell a division of Baker Book House Company, 1982, 92-93.

[7]Lucado, *God Came Near,* page 75.

[8]A. W. Tozer, *The Knowledge of the Holy* (San Francisco: Harper & Row, Publishers, 1961), 90.

WEEK 29
GOD'S HEART FOR THE LOST

DAY 1

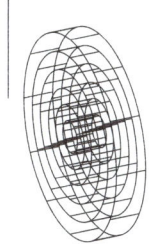

SCRIPTURE MEMORY
Compassion for the Lost
■ **Ezekiel 33:11**
■ **Luke 15:7**
■ **1 Timothy 2:3-4**

"God has a heart, we have a heart, and the secret of our abundant life is receiving his heart into our hearts."[1]

1. Write what the following verses reveal about God's heart.

2 Samuel 14:14

Daniel 9:9

Jonah 4:2

Micah 7:18

2. Who is the object of God's compassion? Why?

Ezekiel 33:11

1 Timothy 2:3-4

2 Peter 3:9

DAY 2

Read Luke 15:1-7.

3. Write your week 16 memory verse ("Christ Is Sinless").

4. Verse 1—Though Christ was sinless, who felt the freedom to come near to Him?

5. What does this tell you about true holiness?

6. Verse 2—Why did the Pharisees and scribes (religious leaders of the day) grumble over Jesus spending time with sinners and taxgatherers?

7. Whom do the 99 sheep represent? (vv. 4-6)

8. Whom does the "one" sheep represent?

9. Does the Shepherd demonstrates a lack of concern for the 99 sheep?

10. According to verse 4, the shepherd ... (check one)

    ❑ waits for the lost sheep to wander back to Him.
    ❑ takes the initiative and searches for the sheep.

11. If a nonbeliever observed your attitude toward him and other nonbelievers what would he conclude about your God? (check one)

    ❑ His shoulders are broad enough to lay another lost sheep upon them.
    ❑ Sorry. His back is only strong enough to shoulder the chosen few.

"Despite the hard-won insights of the centuries that God is one God, world-wide, universal, we keep falling back into the primitive notion that He is local, that He belongs primarily to our tribe, our class, our nation, and that His concern for others beyond our boundaries is lukewarm, or at best exceedingly limited. We have not yet denationalized the God of all nations or grasped the wideness of His love."[2]

12. According to verse 6, the shepherd ... (check one)

    ❑ gets together with his neighbors and friends to talk about how dirty, muddy and stupid the sheep was for leaving the flock.
    ❑ celebrates with neighbors and friends that his sheep has returned home.

13. What kind of ministry is on God's heart? (check one)

    ❑ The kind that stays in the comfort zone of the familiar "sheep."
    ❑ The kind that steps out in pursuit of finding the lost person.

14. Check any of the following that you think Christians sometimes use as excuses not to pursue nonbelievers with the gospel.

    ❑ "They do too many things that I disagree with."
    ❑ "I will just let them see Christ in my lifestyle. If something they see sparks their interest, they'll ask me about it.
    ❑ "To be seen with a non-Christian would hurt my witness."
    ❑ "They can believe the way they want to believe, and I'll believe the way I want to believe.
    ❑ "I'm too busy with the relationships I already have to initiate a relationship with a nonbeliever."

15. Place an "X" beside any of the above statements that you might think or say to keep you from sharing with a nonbeliever.

God has not given us a spirit of timidity, but of power and love and discipline (2 Tim. 1:7).

Read Luke 15:7.

16. What does this verse reveal about the heart of God?

DAY 3

Read Luke 15:8-10.

17. Verse 8—Whom do the 10 coins represent?

18. Whom does the one lost coin represent?

19. Verse 8—What three things does the woman in the parable do to ensure a successful search?

20. How can we apply the same conditions so a lost person may be found?

Light a lamp

Sweep the house

Search carefully

You've probably been in a situation where someone lost her contact lens. Once a person declares the lens missing, it isn't long before everyone around becomes involved in the search. Even strangers often help, too.

21. When would the pursuit of lost souls have a contagious effect upon you to join the search?

22. What does this passage reveal about God's heart for the individual?

23. According to verse 10, what causes the angels to rejoice? (check one)

❑ Bible study
❑ church attendance
❑ seeing a lost person repent
❑ Scripture memory
❑ getting good grades
❑ making a lot of money

24. Write your week 9 memory verse ("The Compassion of God").

25. What are you learning about God's compassion through this study?

DAY 4

Read Nehemiah 9:9-31.

26. Summarize God's provisions for His people when He delivered them from the Egyptians and into the promised land. (vv. 9-15)

27. How did the Israelites rebel against God?

Verse 16

Verse 17

Verse 18

Verse 26

Verse 28

Verse 29

Verse 30

28. How did God respond to the Israelites?

Verse 17

Verse 19

Verse 20

Verse 21

Verse 22

Verse 23

Verse 24

Verse 25

Verse 27

Verse 28

Verse 29

Verse 30

Verse 31

29. In His unceasing forgiveness toward the Israelites, what kind of hope do we see in the heart of God?

30. What impact does this have on you in regard to ...

The lost person on whose salvation you have all but given up.

The backslidden friend who seems unmoved despite your love and prayer efforts.

31. How would you respond to a friend whose reactions to your kindness and goodness could be characterized as rebellious?

32. How does this confirm to you that God is not a man?

DAY 5

In the last four days, we have discovered the longing of God's heart—that the lost would come to know Him. Today we will look at how God's heart impacted the heart of Paul in his own compassion for the lost.

Read Romans 9:1-5.

33. Verse 1—Paul makes three statements that leave little doubt upon the sincerity of what he is about to say. List them.

34. Write down something that you associate with the words *sorrow* and *grief*.

35. Verse 2—To what extent was Paul sorrowful and grief-stricken?

I could wish that I myself were accursed, separated from Christ (Rom. 9:3a).

Is Paul saying that he would give up eternity, exchanging his position in heaven for his brothers' position in hell? Yes. That's exactly what he is saying.

For the sake of my brethren, my kinsman according to the flesh (Rom. 9:3b).

36. Paul's burden was so great for his lost brethren that he would be willing to be punished on their behalf. Who was the Originator of this kind of compassion? Explain.

37. Even though what Paul says here is an impossible scenario—for him to take the place of his brothers in hell—what impresses you about his level of compassion?

38. Paul lists some things that would suggest that from every outward appearance, his brethren should be saved. What are some of the things he mentions? (vv. 4-5)

Think of a person you know that from every outward appearance should be saved (morality, church attendance, generosity, kindness, etc.) yet who is not saved or about whose salvation you are unsure. Pray that you will have the same compassion for him as Paul.

39. What actions will such compassion motivate a Christian to do?

40. Write your week 14 memory verse ("Applying the Word").

Brethren, my heart's desire and my prayer to God for them is for their salvation (Rom. 10:1).

[1] *Lord of the Impossible*, Lloyd John Ogilvie, 1984 Abingdon Press. Used by permission.
[2] J. Wallace Hamilton, *Who Goes There? What and Where Is God?* (Old Tappan: Fleming H. Revell a division of Baker Book House Company, 1958), 126.
[3] Paul E. Billheimer, *Destined for the Throne* (Fort Washington: Christian Literature Crusade, 1975), 63.

WEEK 30
THE WORSHIP OF GOD

DAY 1

SCRIPTURE MEMORY
Worship
■ 1 Chronicles 16:29
■ Ecclesiastes 5:1
■ John 4:24

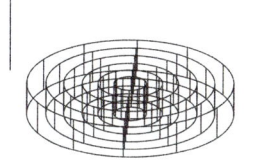

1. Circle the things below that you associate with the word *worship*.

God	Preaching
Hymns	Tithing
Pipe organ	Silence
Praise	Sanctuary
Prayer	Stained glass windows
Music	Responsive readings

Read John 4:19-24.

Today's passage is an excerpt of the conversation between Jesus and the woman at the well. Jesus has just exposed her sin of adultery in verses 17 and 18. The woman changes the subject ...

The woman brings up the controversy of the day between her people–the Samaritans and the Jews. The Jews centered their worship in the temple at Jerusalem. The Samaritans worshipped at Mount Gerizim, even after their temple was destroyed.

2. In Christianity today, can you think of similar "controversies" which detract from true worship? Explain.

3. Verse 21—What does Jesus say about the place of worship?

"Will God indeed dwell on the earth? Behold, heaven and the highest heaven cannot contain Thee, how much less this house which I have built!" (1 Kings 8:27).

"The God who made the world and all things in it, since He is Lord of heaven and earth, does not dwell in temples made with hands" (Acts 17:24).

4. Verse 22—What did Jesus mean by the statement "for salvation is from the Jews"?

"Sir, I perceive that You are a prophet" (v. 19).

What the woman saw when she looked at Jesus was simply a Jew. She did not comprehend that she was in the presence of the true Object of worship–that she was staring Salvation in the face.

"You worship that which you do not know" (v. 22).

5. From your observation of worship, what distracts us from realizing the true Object of our worship?

We are the true circumcision, who worship in the Spirit of God and glory in Christ Jesus and put no confidence in the flesh (Phil. 3:3).

6. Verse 23—In our preconceived ideas, we think that worship is accomplished through our seeking the Lord. Yet, who seeks whom?

A person can only understand God to the extent that God reveals Himself to that individual. God continues to reveal His character (compassion, grace, sovereignty, goodness, justice, love, etc.) to you.

7. How have you been made aware that God has been seeking you to be His true worshiper?

"They come to you as people come, and sit before you as My people, and hear your words, but they do not do them, for they do the lustful desires expressed by their mouth, and their heart goes after their gain. And behold, you are to them like a sensual song by one who has a beautiful voice and plays well on an instrument; for they hear your words, but they do not practice them" (Ezek. 33:31-32).

"This people honors Me with their lips, But their heart is far away from Me. But in vain do they worship Me, Teaching as doctrines the precepts of men" (Matt. 15:8-9).

8. Verse 24—How do the above verses help us to understand what it means to worship in spirit and truth?

9. What is the difference between giving your tithe and giving your life?

10. What is the difference between bowing your head and "bowing your heart"?

11. What is the difference between coming into the sanctuary of a church and coming into the sanctuary of God?

12. Write below what it means to worship in spirit and truth.

DAY 2

Arthur W. Pink writes, "Worship is a redeemed heart *occupied with God*, expressing itself in adoration and thanksgiving."[2]

The Bible itself is a book occupied with God and written by people who were fascinated with Him. Today, as we find ourselves occupied with things other than our Creator and infatuated with things far less worthy than He, we discover our souls in a deep need for the worship expressed and exampled in the Scriptures.

And what book in the Bible more beautifully records the experiences of worship than the Book of Psalms? This is where we will focus our learning of worship today.

Read Psalm 22:22-31.

13. Beside the following verses write what they teach about the worship of God, especially in light of the specific words emphasized next to each reference.

Verse 22—"I will praise Thee"

Verse 23—"Stand in awe"

Verse 27—"Turn to the Lord"
"Worship before Thee"

Verse 29—"Bow before Him"

Verse 31—"Declare His righteousness"

"A Christian's real development in spiritual life will always be revealed by how he or she thinks about God—how much he thinks about Him, and how highly he thinks about Him."[1]
—Sinclair Ferguson

14. Write your week 11 memory verse ("God's Sovereignty").

15. How does verse 28 express God's sovereignty?

16. How does worship bring the calm assurance to your own heart that God is in control of all things?

17. How does worship impact the life of the worshiper in regard to ...

Boldness (v. 22)

Concept of God (v. 24)

Contentment (v. 26)

Lifestyle (v. 27)

18. Who will worship the Lord?

Verse 22

Verse 23

Verse 27

Verse 29

Verses 30-31

19. Check the response that most honestly fills the blank for you. Explain your choice.

It is _____ for me to express to others how I feel about God.

❑ natural   ❑ a joy   ❑ uncomfortable   ❑ terrifying

Read Revelation 4:9-11.

Around the throne were twenty-four thrones; and upon the thrones I saw twenty-four elders sitting, clothed in white garments, and golden crowns upon their heads (Rev. 4:4).

These twenty-four elders represent the entire church of the First-born. This gives us a glimpse of our future participation in worship in heaven—an example we should take seriously in our worship of God while here on earth.

"Thy will be done, On earth as it is in heaven" (Matt. 6:10).

Come, let us worship and bow down; Let us kneel before the Lord our Maker (Ps. 95:6).

20. Describe what comes to mind when you think of "bowing down."

The twenty-four elders will fall down before Him (v. 10a).

21. Why would the following prevent a person from bowing down before the Lord in worship?

Pride

Control

Activities

22. How does "bowing down" impact one's worship of God?

Will cast their crowns before the throne (v. 10b).

23. Describe the picture that comes to mind when you see the word *cast* as used in this verse.

Dan Dehaan writes, "A 'crown' is anything that exalts the wearer."[4]

24. What in your life draws attention to yourself, gives you a sense of value, maybe even a sense of accomplishment? Identify personal crowns which fall in the following categories.

A talent

A friend

A possession

An achievement

Other

"God is continuously being praised. In the realm of eternal and invisible reality, praise is the order of the day. We line up with eternity when we praise."[3]
—Jack R. Taylor

25. Write your week 17 memory verse ("God Is Trustworthy").

26. What risks do you take in trusting these crowns to Christ and casting them before the throne?

27. Write your week 25 memory verse ("Eternal Perspective").

28. How does the worship of God impact your perspective of your crowns?

29. Describe what God is worth to you.

30. Verse 11—How will the elders express to God His worth?

"To receive glory and honor and power" (v. 11).

31. What happens when we seek glory and honor and power for ourselves?

32. According to the last half of verse 11, why is God worthy of these things?

33. Why are we not worthy?

DAY 4

Oswald Chambers writes, "The private relationship of worshipping God is the great essential of fitness ... because in the unseen life which no one saw but God you have become perfectly fit ... 'I can't be expected to live the sanctified life in the circumstances I am in; I have no time for praying just now, no time for Bible reading, my opportunity hasn't come yet; when it does, of course I shall be all right.' No, you will not. If you have not been worshipping as occasion serves, when you get into work you will not only be useless yourself, but a tremendous hindrance to those who are associated with you."[5]

Read 1 Chronicles 16:23-36.

34. Verse 23—What does this verse say to remind us that worshiping God is not to be set aside for the sabbath only?

35. What is true about God according to the following verses?

Verse 25

Verse 26

Verse 27

Verse 34

Tell of His glory among the nations (v. 24).

36. How does the earth and the things that fill the earth "tell" of God's glory?

Verse 30

Verse 31

Verse 32

Verse 33

37. How do the things you just wrote testify of God's glory to all the nations of the earth?

Tell of His glory among the nations (v. 24).

Nature is not the only thing that has been called to "tell" of His glory to the world. As His people, we have also been called to testify.

The word *ascribe* means to "attribute" or "to assign."

38. As His people, how do we "tell of His glory among the nations?"

Verse 28

Verse 29

Verse 35

Verse 36

"Worship the Lord when clothed with holiness!"
(1 Chron. 16:29, TLB).[7]

Every living tree, every roaring sea, every golden field gives glory to God. Some trees may be healthier than others, some fields may be more lush than their neighboring fields; yet, each one glorifies God. It's different for us, though. There may be things in our lives that prevent our testimony of God from being "heard" by the nations.

39. What does verse 29 indicate will hinder our message from getting across to them?

40. How else is our worship different from that of nature's worship?

DAY 5

Read Ecclesiastes 5:1-7.

41. What actions will accompany a person who may have an outward appearance of godliness but who has not really entered into true worship?

Verse 2

Verse 3

Verse 4

Verse 7

42. What perspective will the person who has entered into true worship understand about God?

Verse 2

Verse 4

Verse 7

Draw near to listen rather than to offer (v. 1).

43. Worship should be characterized more by ... (check one)

❏ giving to God.
❏ receiving from God.

"Be Still and Know that I am God: I will be exalted among the heathen, I will be exalted in the earth" (Ps. 46:10, *KJV*).

44. With what does God want to fill your worship experiences?

Guard your steps as you go to the house of God (v. 1)

45. What does Ecclesiastes 5:1 mean to you?

46. As a result of this study, how will your worship experience be different?

[1]*A Heart for God*, Sinclair B. Ferguson, © 1985, 210. Used by Permission of Nav Press/Pinon Press. All rights reserved. For Copies call 1-800-366-7788..

[2]Arthur W. Pink, *Exposition of the Gospel of John, Volume 1* (Swengel: Bible Truth Depot, 1945), 210.

[3]Jack R. Taylor, *The Hallelujah Factor* (Nashville, Tennessee: Broadman Press, 1983), 69.

[4]Taken from *The God You Can Know* by Dan Dehaan, Moody Press, copyright 1982, 2001, 91. Used with permission.

[5]Oswald Chambers, *My Utmost for His Highest* (Westwood: Barbour and Company, Inc., 1935, 1963), 187.

[6]A. W. Tozer, *The Root of the Righteous* (Camp Hill: Christian Publications, 1955, 1986), 130.

[7]Verses marked TLB are taken from *The Living Bible*. Copyright © Tyndale House Publishers, Wheaton, Illinois, 1971. Used by permission.

CONCEPT OF GOD SURVEY

This page should look familiar to you. It is a duplicate copy of the survey you completed before you began this study about understanding and knowing God. Complete this follow-up survey. As before, write down *the first thing that comes to your mind.* When you have completed it, you will want to compare it with your responses to the original survey.

Today's date _____

1. The first word that comes to my mind when I think about God is _____.

2. When I think about God, I feel _____.

3. If I do something I shouldn't have done, God will _____.

4. Sometimes I wish God would _____.

5. The thing I need to change to please God is _____.

6. The thing that frustrates me most about God is _____.

7. God surprises me when _____.

8. One thing I'm afraid God will do is _____.

9. I feel that God wants to take _____ away from me.

10. If God told me to do something I would feel _____.

11. God gives me something so that He _____.

12. I don't think God loves me when _____.

13. God helps me only when I _____.

14. God is farthest away from me when _____.

15. I don't feel God listens to me when I _____.

16. In times of need I don't turn to God because _____.

17. I feel that my problems are _____ for God.

18. I feel God always forgets _____.

19. It is hard for me to pray to God when/because _____.

20. If I made Christ the Lord of my life, then _____.

Concept of God test inspired by Michael Wells, Sidetracked In the Wilderness (Tarrytown: Revell, 1991) pages 58-59.

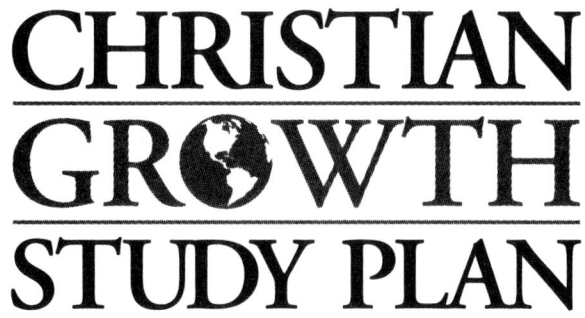

CHRISTIAN GROWTH STUDY PLAN

Preparing Christians to Serve

In the **Christian Growth Study Plan (formerly Church Study Course),** this book *The Discipling Cycle Series: Understanding God* is a resource for course credit in the subject area Personal Life-Youth of the Christian Growth category of plans. To receive credit, youth should attend the 30 study sessions from this book. Duplicate a copy of this form for each student and complete the information. Send the completed page to:

Christian Growth Study Plan
One LifeWay Plaza
Nashville, TN 37234-0117
FAX: (615)251-5067
E-mail: cgspnet@lifeway.com

For information about the Christian Growth Study Plan, refer to the Christian Growth Study Plan Catalog. If is located online at *www.lifeway.com/cgsp.* If you do not have access to the Internet, contact the Christian Growth Study Plan office (1.800.968.5519) for the specific plan you need for your ministry.

The Discipling Cycle Series: Understanding God
CG-0629

PARTICIPANT INFORMATION

Social Security Number (USA ONLY-optional)	Personal CGSP Number*	Date of Birth (MONTH, DAY, YEAR)

Name (First, Middle, Last)	Home Phone

Address (Street, Route, or P.O. Box)	City, State, or Province	Zip/Postal Code

Please check appropriate box: ❑ Resource purchased by self   ❑ Resource purchased by church   ❑ Other

CHURCH INFORMATION

Church Name

Address (Street, Route, or P.O. Box)	City, State, or Province	Zip/Postal Code

CHANGE REQUEST ONLY

☐ Former Name

☐ Former Address	City, State, or Province	Zip/Postal Code

☐ Former Church	City, State, or Province	Zip/Postal Code

Signature of Pastor, Conference Leader, or Other Church Leader	Date

*New participants are requested but not required to give SS# and date of birth. Existing participants, please give CGSP# when using SS# for the first time.
Thereafter, only one ID# is required. Mail to: Christian Growth Study Plan, One LifeWay Plaza, Nashville, TN 37234-0117. Fax: (615)251-5067.

Rev. 3-03